GAME OF DRONES

RICHARD L. MARTINDELL,
LIEUTENANT COLONEL, USAF, RETIRED

CONTENTS

AUTHOR'S NOTE: This manuscript has been reviewed by the Department of Defense Office of Prepublication to ensure no classified information has been compromised.

**CLEARED AS AMENDED
For Open Publication**

Sep 27, 2022

Department of Defense
OFFICE OF PREPUBLICATION AND SECURITY REVIEW

It was also reviewed by General Atomics Systems Integration to ensure no company intellectual property or proprietary information has been revealed. The following disclaimer is required by General Atomics:

DISCLAIMER

The views expressed in this publication are those of the author and do not necessarily reflect the views of General Atomics.

PROLOGUE

It was the day before my seventieth birthday when I stepped off the plane at Al Asad Air Base, Iraq, to help fight ISIS, the Taliban, and whoever else was fomenting trouble in the Middle East. This story relates how I got here and places I went after that.

I flew my last combat sortie in an F-4 from Korat, Thailand, to Cambodia on July 1, 1973, attacking North Vietnamese supply lines to South Vietnam. Flying drones in Iraq was going to be a different experience.

While the efficacy of drones is obvious to me, I had been a longtime critic of the Air Force integration of remotely piloted aircraft (RPAs) into the force structure in terms of selecting, assigning, and handling personnel involved with flying unmanned aerial vehicles (UAVs) or drones. It seemed criminal to me to take a newly minted pilot straight out of pilot training and assign him or her to flying drones. Actually, it seemed mean to assign anybody to fly drones. I thought it would be better to let a person get some experience and maturity flying manned aircraft before sending them to fly drones. Another problem for people who got assigned to fly drones was the fact that, early on, they were producing drones faster than the Air Force could produce pilots and sensor operators, so once assigned to fly drones, it was hard to break out of that community and get back into manned aircraft. Fortunately for the Air Force, I had no conduit to voice my dissatisfaction with what I thought was poor management of resources. I also had no ability to influence anybody in this area.

Those of us who flew combat missions in Southeast Asia during the Vietnam conflict also heard of drone crews suffering from the stress of flying drones. Us old heads had a hard time understanding how it could be stressful flying a drone from a control van that wasn't going to suffer any injuries if the drone got shot down. The reasons for post-traumatic stress disorder (PTSD) for drone crews were explained to me by people who had been there and done that, and they made sense. The oversight and scrutiny when flying drones were intense. Those of us who dropped bombs from F-4s and F-105s rarely saw the actual death and destruction we created. Drone crews saw it every day because they had to monitor their targets to get permission to strike those targets, and then they watched them explode on their video displays. Supervisors and intelligence observers could easily identify collateral damage and assign blame. So while there was no threat of being shot down, needing to try to escape and evade on the ground, or the possibility of being captured as a prisoner of war, there were other mental challenges to deal with. Another drone pilot told me of the dichotomy of having breakfast with his wife and children before sending the kids to school and then driving to the base, getting in the control van, and being interjected into the combat operations halfway around the world since the drones in Afghanistan and Iraq were remotely piloted from bases in Nevada, California, and other stateside locations.

Finally, media reports of the conflicts in Afghanistan and Iraq seemed inadequate for two reasons: the media's basic aversion to the military and their ignorance of military operations, which lead to their inability to accurately report the situation. I wanted to know what was really going on. I appreciated military speakers who briefed military affiliated organizations I belonged to, but it was still secondhand knowledge. I wanted a way to see for myself.

My journey to Iraq started at a monthly luncheon with eight or ten fellow pilots at the Casa Machado restaurant at Montgomery Field in San Diego in October 2017. At our monthly luncheons, we solved many world problems among ourselves. The solutions we came up with went no further than the table where we were sitting as our six degrees of influence didn't reach national policymakers.

I had been working for John and Martha King at King Schools for eleven years, developing pilot training courses starting as a contract subject matter expert (SME) then getting hired as a full-time course developer and SME and working my way up in the organization to become the vice president of course development, with several flight instructors working for me to develop and maintain our courses. Our courses needed constant updating, thanks to changes in the FAA regulations. However, there was no more progression available for me, and the job was getting stale.

At our lunch meeting in October, the subject of drones came up, and one of the pilots said a friend of his at General Atomics told him General Atomics needed drone pilots to support the military because the military couldn't generate enough pilots internally to meet their operational needs. General Atomics wanted civilian pilots with a commercial pilot's certificate, an instrument rating, the ability to get an FAA second-class medical certificate, at least five hundred hours of pilot-in-command time, and the ability to get a secret security clearance with the military. I met all those requirements, so I looked at the job opportunities on the General Atomics website, found an open position for a deployable pilot, and applied. A positive for me was that I wouldn't have to relocate. I could live anywhere and deploy from that location once I was qualified. Within forty-eight hours, I got an automated, polite "Thanks, but no, thanks" e-mail. I e-mailed the contact in General Atomics (GA) and told him I applied but was rejected. He reassured me that was the nature of the GA human resources system. He said I should apply for every listed pilot position and keep applying. I went back to the GA website, found five positions for deployable pilots, and applied for all of them. Within forty-eight hours, I got four more "no-thank-yous" and one "We'd like to talk, please respond to schedule a telephone interview."

The telephone interview in early December was very straightforward, and all the HR person wanted to do was verify the information on my application. Shortly after the telephone interview, I got a phone call saying they would like to do an in-person interview and would fly me into Los Angeles or Ontario from San Diego and arrange a rental car and a hotel in Palmdale or Victorville for an interview at their flight operations facility.

I wanted to schedule an interview after the holidays in January, and I asked if I could just fly myself into their flight operations facility. That threw her for a loop. She said she'd have to check to see if that was possible. She called back a day later to say that I couldn't land at their facility, so I said I'd fly into the airport at Victorville, California. She said there wasn't any commercial service into Victorville, still not comprehending I planned to fly myself in a rental airplane. Once we got that straightened out, she said no problem, they would arrange a rental car for me at the Victorville airport to get to their flight operations facility.

As the day for the interview in January approached, the weather was questionable, so I called to ask if they could arrange a hotel for me, and I would drive myself up from San Diego the day before the interview and then drive back to San Diego after the interview. The travel coordinator was happy to handle the changes, and I was on my way.

When I got to the GA-ASI flight operations facility, I checked in with security and was directed to a trailer, where the interviews would take place. First up was the HR person I had been talking with on the phone to make all the arrangements, and again, all she wanted to do was go over my application and verify the information. When she got done and asked if I had any questions, I asked when a hiring decision would be made. To my surprise, she said, "Today." This was a refreshing change compared with the multiple interview-hiring process at King Schools. Next up was one of the actual pilot managers, who asked about my background. He was a former Navy pilot and appreciated my F-4 and F-15 experience. He wanted to know if I could qualify for a second-class FAA medical certificate. I already had one so that was off the table. There was never any discussion of my age, thanks to antidiscrimination rules, even though it was clearly on my application. Another question was if I thought I'd have any trouble getting a secret security clearance. Since I had previously held a top-secret clearance, I didn't think there would be a problem renewing my clearance to secret. The interview was on a Thursday, and he wanted to know when I had last flown. He smiled when I said, "The day before yesterday." They had been getting a lot of applicants who met the qualifications but were not currently flying. When we got done, he said the HR person would be back to give me an offer letter and set up a start date. Boom, end of process! I wanted to give a month's notice to King Schools rather than the standard two weeks, and I wanted to take some time off before starting my training at GA-ASI's flight operations facility. We agreed on a start date in April, contingent on a successful background check. Then I drove ten miles from one GA-ASI flight operations facility to another to visit security, start the background check, and get instructions to complete the application for a secret security clearance. After that, I headed back to San Diego. I submitted my resignation letter to King Schools the following day. I was eager to start a new adventure.

CHAPTER 1

Spring 2018

THE HIGH DESERT

If you have seen the movie *The Right Stuff* or read about Air Force flight testing, you have heard of California's High Desert. The High Desert and Edwards Air Force Base are the home of all that has been and is new and exciting in Air Force flight test and evaluation.

Driving north out of San Bernardino on Interstate 15 through the Cajon Pass to the High Desert of Southern California felt like déjà vu all over again. Forty-seven years earlier, I drove the same interstate on my way to George Air Force Base near Victorville to learn to fly the F-4 Phantom. Now I'm driving to Palmdale to learn to fly the MQ-9 Reaper.

At the time, General Atomics trained pilots and systems operators at several locations strategically but inconveniently located in the middle of nowhere: Dugway, Utah; Waco, Texas; Grand Forks, North Dakota;[28] and the High Desert of Southern California, for example. In Southern California's desert, there are actually two facilities about halfway between Victorville and Palmdale.

GA-ASI's Southern California desert facilities are bleak. Prefab hangars and buildings and office trailers are plopped down in the middle of a dusty desert plain.

The first look reminded me of a modern-day Western boom town. The only things lacking were horses, hitching posts, and saloons. A stockyard feeding lot lay just southeast of the facility, so if the wind was blowing the right direction, you got the aroma of the Old West as well. Very little other than the runways, aircraft parking ramps, and roads in and out of each facility were paved. Only the cars and satellite dishes told you it was not the 1800s.

The people made it seem like the Wild West too: burly, gruff many men with full beards; men and women with prolific tattoos abounded; conforming nonconformists. Despite the outward appearance of roughness, everyone was friendly, helpful, and professional.

I considered myself fortunate to be training at this location as it was just a three-hour drive from my home in San Diego. My instructions were to check into the Marriott Residence Inn in Palmdale on Sunday and expect to be there for five months. I was to report for new hire orientation Monday morning at six o'clock at GA-ASI's flight operations facility. Workdays were nine hours a day for four days then eight hours on the first Friday. The next week you worked nine hours a day, Monday through Thursday then Friday off, giving us a three-day weekend for each two-week pay period.

The thirtymile drive from Palmdale to GA-ASI's flight operations facility takes about forty minutes. I would get to know that drive well over the next five months.

For me, that forty minutes meant a 5:00 a.m. departure from the hotel. There were several of us in the lobby Monday morning, getting ready to make our individual drives. Our first stop at GA-ASI's flight operations facility was the security office at the entrance gate to get our identification badges to access the facilities. Once in the classroom for orientation, there were sixteen people. Three of us were aircrew, and the rest were new engineers, aircraft maintenance technicians, administrators, and other support personnel. The day consisted of briefings from human resources, payroll, deployment coordinators, and others.

It was here I learned I would be flying MQ-9s for the Air Force rather than MQ-1s or MQ-9s for the Army. This was another stroke of good luck. The person from the deployment department explained that when you deployed to an overseas Army location, you first reported to Fort Bliss in El Paso, Texas, for a painful week of orientation training before getting on either a military transport or a military charter jet to fly to your deployment location. On the other hand, if you were deploying to fly for the Air Force, the General Atomics travel department simply coordinated airline tickets from the commercial airport of your choice nearest your home to a commercial airport near your deployment site and then provided ground or air transportation to your deployment location. This reinforced what I had observed in twenty-one years of military service. The Air Force did a better job of treating people like humans rather than cattle.

While the MQ-1[29] and the MQ-9[30] are similar in appearance, they are also substantially different. The MQ-1 is a two-thousand-pound aircraft powered by a Rotax engine that uses gas, and the MQ-9 is a ten-thousand-pound aircraft powered by a turbo-prop engine that uses jet fuel. Both aircraft have four cameras: two day-TV cameras and two infrared (IR) cameras. One day-TV and one IR camera each is fixed in the nose, providing a forward view for the pilot to use day or night. The other day-TV and IR cameras are in a ball turret under the nose of the aircraft that can be aimed to look at points of interest on the ground. Both aircraft can carry various air-to-ground weapons, but the MQ-9 can carry more than the MQ-1. Under the rules of the Geneva Convention, only military aircrew can employ the weapons the aircraft carry. Civilian crews are restricted to flying surveillance and reconnaissance missions only. When we fly surveillance and reconnaissance missions, we position the aircraft and point the cameras where our military controller tells us. The Geneva Convention prohibits civilians from making targeting decisions. These rules were strongly stressed in our academics on tactical employment and the laws of armed conflict.

Even though the MQ-9 is bigger and heavier than the MQ-1, they look a lot alike. The easiest way to distinguish between the two is to look at the tail of the aircraft. If the stabilators look like a "V," it's an MQ-9. If the stabilators look like an inverted "V" (∧), it's an MQ-1. There's also a lot of discussion about what to call these things. Some well-intended people say the word "drone" is insensitive and derogatory. It's a perfectly good word that is simple and readily understood by the general public. Some people are overly concerned about being politically incorrect. People in the industry refer to them as drones as well. Others like the term UAV for unmanned aerial vehicle, trying to make it sound more official and formal, but it ignores the fact that even though the vehicle is unmanned, there is much human involvement to fly the aircraft. A similar term is UAS for unmanned aerial system that includes not only the aircraft but also the control station and the communications link between the two. The military uses RPV for remotely piloted vehicle, which is more accurate to me in that it acknowledges the fact that a pilot is involved, even if he or she is not in the aircraft. They are communicating with the aircraft to control it. All the terms can be used interchangeably.

The pilots and sensor operators training to fly the aircraft are an eclectic bunch. Pilots come from various sources, including those who had been instructors in flight schools and others who had a commercial pilot certificate with the bare minimum requirement of five hundred hours pilot-in-command time as well as pilots who flew drones in the military. Many sensor operators came straight from the military, and others came from formal flight training programs at places like Embry-Riddle and the University of North Dakota. Some of the staff were prior military pilots like me, but I was the only one in the training program at the time. I tried to stay low key about my background but answered honestly when asked what I had flown. The fact that I had flown F-4s and F-15s meant I had tactical experience, but like everyone else, I was a fledgling learning to fly UAVs. While everyone seemed to be a gamer, the sensor operators, in particular, are very computer-savvy. Many of the pilots and sensor operators are younger and were using this job effectively to pay off college debts. Deployment pay is very good, and if you don't have a car or house payment, your expenses are negligible, so savings would accrue quickly. While everyone was motivated to learn and to accomplish the mission, a few seemed to me to be what most of us would consider typical millennials. As an example of their self-indulgence, the Residence Inn most of us were staying at was probably ten or fifteen years old. When a newer long-term hotel opened nearby, many began to complain, coming up with excuses of why they needed to move to the newer facility with "better" accommodations. The fact is our-home-away-from-home was just fine. The inn had a pool, an exercise room, and served heavy hors d'oeuvres Monday, Tuesday, and Wednesday evenings, as well as giving us a complimentary breakfast. For those of us who had to leave the hotel before the breakfast bar opened, they arranged for us to have a takeout hot or cold breakfast selection. All in all, the staff and facilities were very accommodating. The folks who wangled a move to the newer hotel later regretted the decision because of the poorer service at the new facility. Karma.

No program to support the government would be complete without paperwork. Before any of us could start training, we had to get approval from the Air Force for each of us to enter the training program. This involved a detailed form listing your flying experience and qualifications—a form that had to be filled out in *exactly* the manner prescribed by the Air Force. Once the form was complete, the approval process would take about two weeks. The administrative team in the training department guided us through the form to make sure it met Air Force specifications before they submitted it to the on-site Air Force representative to approve our entry into the training program and authorize us to fly military assets at the facilities.

During the two weeks it took to get approval to start formal training, we had plenty of computer courses to take to satisfy all the administrative requirements of being employed in California. We struggled through payroll procedures, sexual harassment training, applying for medical insurance, and a multitude of other courses with absolutely no guidance on a good sequence on how to get through the maze. On top of that, we were given flight manuals and aircraft study sheets to review before we started training and told to start memorizing aircraft systems limitations, also with no guidance on how to attack the mountain of information. Finally, we were shown where all the academic lessons for the aircraft were located on the local computer server and told we could start studying those PowerPoint presentations.

It takes two people to fly and operate an MQ-1 or MQ-9: the pilot who flies the aircraft and the sensor operator (SO), who manipulates the cameras in the sensor ball in the chin dome. There are two levels of qualification for flying either aircraft for pilots and sensor operators. The first is called mission command element (MCE), and the second is launch-and-recovery element (LRE).[31] MCE is the easier of the two qualifications and is the first level of training for everyone. Launch-and-recovery pilots and SOs get training on takeoffs and landings once they are MCE-qualified. On a normal flight, which can last up to twenty hours, the LRE, located on the airfield where the drone is based, will get the aircraft airborne and then hand it off to the mission crew who will fly the mission. The mission crew can be colocated at the launch-and-recovery base or anywhere in the world. The mission crew flies the aircraft using a datalink through a satellite. Once the mission is over, the mission crew hands the aircraft back to a launch-and-recovery crew, who land the aircraft back at the base where they and the drone are stationed. A typical mission situation is for a launch crew to launch an aircraft in Iraq or Afghanistan, hand the aircraft off to a mission crew somewhere in the United States, who then takes over the control of the aircraft. After fifteen or more hours, the mission crew returns to the base where they took off, and another LRE crew lands the aircraft. During the mission, MCE crews will take turns flying the aircraft in shifts, and the crew that lands the airplane will likely not be the same crew that launched it because of shift-changes at the base of operations.

The Aeronautical Systems division of General Atomics, called General Atomics-ASI, builds the MQ-1 and MQ-9. They are a manufacturing organization that produces a product and were never intended to be a training organization producing pilots and systems operators. This became painfully apparent as I progressed through the training program. The people ASI hired to create a training program copied the best pilot training program available. The syllabus for learning to fly drones looked just like the syllabus I used to train pilots to fly the F-15 when I was in the Air Force. There were three training events: academics, simulators, and flights. Before you could do anything in or with the aircraft, you had to do it on a simulator, and before you could do something on the simulator, you had to have the necessary academics to understand what you were trying to do on the simulator before you moved on to the aircraft.

The mission pilot syllabus showed a course flow of about fifty training days or approximately two and a half calendar months. I didn't understand why I was told I would be in training for five months, but as time passed, the reason became clear. They didn't have enough instructors available to handle the number of students they were trying to train. The instructors they did have were also subject to deployment and, therefore, not available to teach when they were deployed. Training was feast or famine. Looking at the syllabus, I could easily see what academic lessons I needed to accomplish before the next simulator event, so I would study the appropriate PowerPoint lessons then wait for an instructor who could teach them. I would go days with no lessons scheduled and then would have three or four scheduled on a single day. The quality of instruction also varied. Some instructors just read the PowerPoint slides, and others would actually explain what the slide was trying to teach. Explaining the information in the lessons was very effective and beneficial since the PowerPoint lessons were developed by the engineers responsible for designing that particular system, not teachers. Because the PowerPoints were developed by engineers, the lessons on the various systems were excruciatingly detailed. It felt like they were trying to teach you how to build each system rather than how to use it. Instructors who took the time to give you practical information about a given system or topic were greatly appreciated.

My first simulator experience showed me the most challenging human factors engineering I had ever seen. I had been formally trained as a flight safety officer by the Air Force, and what I saw violated many of the design criteria I had learned about human factors and what made for a good man-machine interface. The pilot and systems operator control stations seemed to be designed by engineers for engineers, with little apparent consideration given to previously proven display conventions in manned aircraft. By necessity, a lot of information needs to be passed from the control station to the aircraft, but just as critical and ongoing, information needs to be passed from the aircraft to the control station to be monitored and used to autonomously fly the aircraft as well as view the videos from the sensors. Since engineers revel in data, they made sure every single piece of information coming from the aircraft could be monitored in the control van by the pilot and sensor operator as well as technicians at stations in the van with the flying crew. The problem is that, normally, it's way too much information, so much more than the pilot normally needs to fly the airplane. Temperatures, pressures, voltages, and amperages from a myriad of components produced information overload, yet the engineers wanted to make sure all the data was available at the console. Consequently, nearly a hundred different screens can be viewed with scads of data on each screen. But only one or two salient pieces of information are found on most screens. On top of that, the information was in tabular data format rather than easy-to-read and interpreted gauges. The only way to access a particular screen is to know the page number of that screen so you can manually type it into the display system to bring that screen up to be viewed.

From a pilot's perspective, there are situational-awareness features common in manned aircraft, even relatively inexpensive small civilian planes, that could have easily been incorporated into the software for these drones, but those features were either considered and dismissed or the designers were ignorant of them. Like most modern aircraft, there was an annunciation screen that displayed warnings when a system was out of tolerance or malfunctioning. It would have been easy to have the checklist for any malfunction automatically displayed on one of the other monitors available in the control van, but that efficiency step was not built into the system. Likewise, useful information that is routinely shown on manned aircraft displays could have been available on similar displays in the control van. A simple example is that on electronic flight displays in manned aircraft, the pilot can set bugs on the airspeed indicator to show rotation speed, best angle-of-climb speed, best rate-of-climb speed, and best glide speed. That feature doesn't exist on any of the displays for the pilot in the control van. The only speed that is constantly displayed is stall speed. What's really sad is that with all the information the engineers have, from the aircraft pumping down to the control van, those other speeds could also easily be calculated for the given aircraft weight and atmospheric conditions then automatically displayed without the pilot needing to manually search for and enter the speeds.

On the other hand, and despite my criticisms of the engineers and their man-machine interface, the MQ-9 is an amazing engineering accomplishment. The design builds in a lot of safeguards so the pilot can't fly the aircraft beyond its capabilities. Since the pilot is not in the aircraft, there is no "seat-of-the-pants" feel for what the airplane is doing, so the software prevents you from putting the aircraft out of control.

As we got into the academic training, when classes were scheduled, they frequently began at 6:00 a.m., so it was convenient to get to work at 5:00 a.m., and that meant a 3:45 a.m. get-up. Even in the summer, with daylight savings time, it was dark for the drive to work. That early call may sound bad, but there was no problem getting to work that early. What surprised me was the amount of traffic at that hour on the road going into Palmdale as I drove out of Palmdale to GA-ASI's flight operations facility. Another benefit of getting to work that early was avoiding morning rush-hour traffic going to the Lockheed facilities at Air Force Plant 42, known as the Palmdale Airport. The same was true for getting off work early in the afternoon and missing the normal evening rush hour.

The MQ-9, like any aircraft, flies better in cooler air than hot air, so the flights were scheduled to take off at six thirty in the morning. Briefings for flights were a standard two hours before takeoff. To be ready to brief at four thirty, I had to leave the hotel no later than three thirty. Our supervisor did us a favor and transferred us to the swing shift rather than the day shift, so we had to report to work no later than four o'clock each morning, even if we weren't scheduled to fly. One benefit of that change was a pay raise brought about by the shift differential. Another benefit for me was that on our three-day weekends, I was able to leave for San Diego just after lunch on Thursday, giving me two full days in San Diego to help my daughter-in-law take care of her two girls, a pleasant task and one made important as my son was deployed to Iraq flying Scan Eagle drones for the Navy. I was also able to stop at March Air Reserve Base just outside Riverside, which was exactly halfway between Palmdale and San Diego. I could fly T-34s in the March aero club and maintain my pilot proficiency flying by myself and in formation with friends.

Besides the normal systems knowledge about hydraulics, engine, and electrical systems, there were two areas unique to drones that had to be learned. The first involved the various command and control links between the control van, called the ground control station (GCS), and the aircraft. During takeoffs and landings, line-of-sight C-band frequencies are used.

If you will be operating at longer ranges, it is necessary to start controlling the drone using a satellite data link.

Once you have the theory down, it's time to start flying, and to do that, you need to understand the flight control system. Since there is no pilot on board, an autopilot is always flying the aircraft. You need to learn the three different ways the pilot on the ground can tell the autopilot in the aircraft what to do. First, there is a manual or hand-flying mode, which is much like flying a manned aircraft. The throttle, control stick, and rudder pedals control airspeed, attitude, and altitude. You turn the aircraft by moving the control stick left or right, and you dive or climb by moving the control stick fore and aft. This mode is used mostly in the traffic pattern for takeoffs and landings. Once you get underway to your mission area, you can engage the hold modes. When you use the hold modes, you set or command heading hold to maintain a heading, altitude hold to maintain an altitude, and airspeed hold to maintain an airspeed. New values can be commanded for any of the parameters using the computer keyboard, then the autopilot will make the aircraft fly the new heading, altitude, or airspeed.

Somewhere halfway through my training, I got put on the deployment schedule. The powers that be projected a date when I would finish my training and get a qualification check flight. My tentative deployment date was early November. I would go to Al Asad Air Base in Iraq. This was exactly the assignment I had been hoping for when I applied for the job. I wanted to see firsthand what was going on in our efforts in the Middle East.

Once I got heavily into the flight training portion of the program, the scheduling irregularities did not get any better. On two occasions, I went two weeks without being scheduled to do anything. So I sat around and reviewed the academic lessons. After one two-week period of not doing anything, I was scheduled to fly four mornings in a row, which gave me very little time to get to the simulator to practice what I had just been taught on a flight. The pilot in me did not appreciate the lack of continuity in the training. Unlike my pervious Air Force training, where all the simulators you needed to complete the program were built into the schedule, here, you were expected to get simulator time on your own, in addition to the syllabus-required simulator training to practice anything you wanted to reinforce. I often felt I wanted more than I was getting in the training. In the back of my mind, I knew that the program was designed to have you succeed, so while I might not be getting as much training and information as I wanted, I knew I was getting the information I needed to be able to do the job and pass the check ride. If you weren't stupid or dangerous, you *would* graduate from the training program.

Prior to deploying, there were additional computer-based training modules that had to be accomplished for the Air Force. That training included additional communications and operational security lessons, cultural awareness, the civilian equivalent of the code of conduct, and how to handle yourself should you become a political prisoner. I used my down time between being scheduled for flights to get through that training, and as time passed, it was a good thing that I did.

Somewhere in early August, my departure date got moved up thirty days to early October. Our team at Al Asad was flying MQ-1s for the Air Force, and they were scheduled to transition to MQ-9s. I would be part of the first team of MQ-9 pilots. No surprise, we had to be in place in Al Asad before the aircraft got there. Based on where I was in the training program and how scheduling had been going, I thought this earlier date was optimistic. It would require aggressive scheduling to complete the program that quickly, but that was the company's problem to solve, not mine. By mid-August, my deployment date got changed again to late September because of the lack of availability of company charter flights in October to get to Al Asad from the nearest commercial airport in Erbil, Iraq.

My flight out of San Diego was scheduled for Sunday, September 23rd, There was little doubt in my mind that I would pass my check ride when I flew it on September 12th, based not only on the training I received but also on the fact the company was out of time, if they wanted me to make my scheduled deployment date. I still had to shepherd my paperwork through the administrative process to get me authorized to fly Air Force aircraft operationally, as well as get my visa to be in Iraq. My passport had been sent to the Iraqi Embassy, to get the visa in August, and it still hadn't come back. The passport finally arrived Tuesday, September 18th. I finished up the rest of the administrative paperwork and left Palmdale for San Diego on Wednesday September 19th to pack and get ready to leave on Sunday. The full itinerary was to fly from San Diego to London overnight on British Airways. Monday morning, I would change planes in London and continue to Vienna, Austria, where I would spend the night at the hotel at the airport. Tuesday, I would fly from Vienna to Erbil, Iraq, on Austrian Airways and spend the night in company contract quarters. Wednesday morning, I would take the company charter flight from Erbil to Al Asad.

MQ-9 Control Station (USAF Photo)

MQ-1 Predator (USAF Photo)

The High Desert
(Photo courtesy of ForeFlight, A Boeing Company)

MQ-9 Reaper (USAF Photo)

CHAPTER 2

Fall 2018

AL ASAD AIR BASE, IRAQ

2.1 Getting There

After completing my initial training and qualification checks, it was time to make my first deployment in September 2018. Most departures from San Diego pass over Point Loma, straight out over the Pacific Ocean, then turn left, climbing all the while to pass back over the city. Looking down at the valley and reservoir near my home, I was eager to start this adventure. The trip to Al Asad, Iraq, was relatively uneventful as I was able to sleep on the British Airways overnight flight from San Diego to London. The four-hour layover in London, transferring to the flight to Vienna, seemed to go quickly. Even with no bags to carry, it took an hour and a bus to get from the arrival terminal to the departure terminal, and security being security, it was once more through the screening line and metal detector because I changed terminals. Good news, though: In the departure terminal, I found time to sit down for a nice midday meal. Then on to the gate to board the three-hour flight to Vienna. In Vienna, I reclaimed my two seventy-pound checked bags to clear customs and immigration. The rollers on the heavy duffel bags made the half-mile hike from the terminal to the hotel through a pedestrian tunnel manageable. Unfortunately, it was too late to find a good Austrian restaurant, so I settled for an evening meal in the hotel lounge. I had hoped to have something traditionally Austrian, like schnitzel or stroganoff, but wound up with a microwaved lasagna and my last glass of wine for three months.

The next morning came early as I was coping with the time zone changes. I lugged my bags back to the terminal to check in for the flight. The ticket on British Airways from San Diego to Vienna allowed two checked bags, but the ticket on Austrian Airways from Vienna to Erbil, Iraq, only included one checked bag, so I had to go to a separate check-in to pay €100 for the extra bag, claimed on my expense report. After that, I went to the regular passenger check-in. Fortunately, I started the process early and was not rushed for time.

The instructions provided by our travel team said I would be met at the airport in Erbil by a representative from the charter company that would fly us from Erbil to Al Asad. He would have the typical greeter card with the word "PAX" on it so as not to advertise who we were. He would take us to a contract lodging facility on the US military area of the airfield to spend the night before catching the charter flight the next morning. That turned out to be old information—and bad information. He had no sign. He simply looked for lost souls in the arrival hall then quietly asked, "Are you with General Atomics?" Unfortunately, he missed me and another GA employee. The two of us hired a cab to take us from the terminal to the military compound. There, we found a phone and called our site leader at Al Asad to say we were roaming around looking for our connection to get to the contract quarters and on our flight. The site leader at Al Asad called his replacement who was on the same flight we were on. We connected at the dining facility, had dinner, and checked into the overnight quarters. Next morning, the charter flight representative took the three of us and about twelve other contractor personnel back to the terminal to clear security and immigration, even though it was a domestic flight. Then we boarded the Beech 1900 for the one-hour flight to Al Asad. The Beech 1900 is a twin-engine turbo-prop aircraft that carries nineteen passengers in a cramped seating arrangement, with window seats on each side of the aircraft and a single aisle between them.

2.2 KBR

Kellogg, Brown, Root & Wiley, known simply as KBR, contracts with the government to provide services and civil engineering support on military bases in the Middle East. An American psychologist named Abraham Maslow identified seven needs for humans to survive. They are air, safety, clothing, food, water, shelter, and sleep. KBR provides food, water, and shelter for sleeping.

When you get off the airplane at Al Asad, the site lead meets you and takes you to the KBR billeting office, where you are assigned your room for the next three months. Housing comes in the form of prefabricated containerized housing units called CHUs (pronounced chews). Each CHU has three ten-foot-by-fifteen-foot rooms, and there are approximately twenty CHUs per revetted block, meaning there's a barrier of twenty feet tall concrete T-wall sections around the group of CHUs. Our housing area, called Tripoli, had ten blocks of twenty CHUs. There are multiple housing areas located all around the base. Each ten-foot-by-fifteen-foot room in a CHU has two bunkbeds and two standing lockers. I was fortunate as my room also had a chair and a desk. You share the room with one other person, who is on the opposite shift that you are on. Since your work schedule is twelve hours on and twelve hours off, seven days a week, you each have the room to yourself while the other person is working. Shift-change occurs at 4:00 a.m. for the day crew going on and 4:00 p.m. for the night crew going to work.

There's no running water in the room. Communal showers and restrooms are located just outside the concrete barriers for each block of CHUs. There is a separate male latrine prefab building and male shower prefab building. The female building has latrines and showers in it and is secured by a cypher lock. That combination, obviously, is known only to the women.

In addition to the quarters, KBR is responsible for maintaining and cleaning the shower and lavatory facilities daily. The shower and latrine facilities smell of disinfectant, more than just a fresh clean smell. The commode stalls are smaller than any lavatory on an airliner. When you close the door, your knees are in your face and touching the door. On the other hand, we aren't complaining. These were a better option than the international port-a-potties on the rest of the base in the operational and administrative areas. An international port-a-potty is one that has places for your feet on either side of the seat so you can squat over the hole rather than sit on the seat as is common in the Middle East.

The shower stalls are private but barely big enough to turn around in. When I was in high school, no one worried about being in communal showers and toweling off in front of your locker. Now everybody is sensitive about being naked in front of others since you don't know the sexual orientation of the other people in the facility, Which brings up the subject of water. Whatever water and sewer systems existed on base before Desert Storm are no longer functional. Any facility with running water has one or more five-thousand-gallon fresh water supply tanks and an equal number of wastewater tanks. KBR operates a fleet of tanker trucks that supply fresh water and remove wastewater. These trucks operate 24/7 to keep up with the demand of all the personnel. Needless to say, they are clearly labeled as being potable or wastewater trucks.

While the facilities are certainly adequate, looking back, I appreciated my living accommodations in Thailand for my one year flying combat missions in Southeast Asia more than the facilities at Al Asad. In Thailand, the comparable housing unit, called a hooch, had four ten-foot-by-twenty-foot rooms, also with two people in a room. The room had a divider that made half the room the sleeping area and the other half the living area. In Thailand, our living areas had two desks and all the stereo equipment we accumulated during our year in country. In the middle of the structure, with two rooms on either side, was a common day room adjacent to the latrine and shower facilities. Each squadron had a separate hooch area that was landscaped with grass and palm and rubber trees. While the individual rooms were air-conditioned, the day room and bathroom facilities were not. At Al Asad, the CHUs were situated on gravel areas surrounded by concrete T-walls. One of my strong memories of the facilities in Thailand was my daily satisfaction of seeing my face in the mirror as I shaved. This confirmed I was in Thailand and not a prisoner in North Vietnam. My big satisfaction in Iraq was simply the refreshing shower each morning after a good night's sleep. Small pleasures are important in austere conditions.

Al Asad had three dining facilities, called DFACs, located near various housing and work areas on the base. The main dining facility was located on the north side of the base in what would be considered the administrative area. All food was prepared in the main dining facility then catered to the other two facilities for serving. Four meals were available daily: breakfast, lunch, dinner, and the midnight meal, which had a breakfast line and a dinner line. I usually ate at the dining facility adjacent to my housing area but would occasionally eat at one of the other dining halls just for a change of scenery. The food was mediocre at best.

There was no reason for KBR to be good as there were no other options for dining. KBR had an absolute monopoly. So every day we were treated to a practical example of why socialism doesn't instill excellence. In fact, their main incentive was to minimize expenses while meeting the terms of the contract. There were three entrées to choose from, which were usually some kind of overcooked meat with a variety of sauces sometimes disguised as Mexican, Italian, or Asian cuisine. When they did have steaks, they were like shoe leather. Occasionally, they did a really good job with a pork or beef roast. All the vegetables were canned and the texture of mush. The only things that were fresh were the self-serve sandwich and salad bars. One bright spot for me was Friday evening, when they served steamed crab legs. Tuesdays were pizza day. The pizzas looked like they came from the frozen aisle at the grocery store. They looked so bad I never tried them.

In Thailand, in addition to the military dining facilities, we had the option of going to the Thai restaurant on base, which met US health standards, or driving our flight surgeon crazy by going off base to local restaurants. Even better, in Germany, there was always a German canteen on base and a multitude of good restaurants off base. Likewise, there were plenty of dining options in Italy and Spain, when we deployed there.

To their credit, KBR served thousands of meals during the two- to three-hour window for each meal. They also had expanded menus on holidays like Thanksgiving and Christmas. This was not out of the goodness of their hearts but because it was written in the service contract.

KBR services included self-serve laundromats in each housing area as well as a drop-off laundry service. I did my laundry for the first month. It was a hassle. The facilities were always busy, and to compound the problem, there was an equal number of dryers and washers, this despite the fact that it takes only thirty minutes to wash a load of laundry but it takes sixty minutes to dry that same load, so there was usually a backlog of people waiting for dryers. Doing your laundry required a minimum of an hour and a half of dedicated time but normally closer to two hours. The drop-off laundry service was provided at no charge and only took twenty-four hours to return your clothes. Because of my schedule, it took forty-eight hours to get my laundry back since I was always at work when the clothes were ready to be picked up. Still, it was much more convenient than doing it myself. A big plus was that the clothes came back neatly folded. I took advantage of the drop-off service for the rest of my deployment.

When I dealt with individuals, I found that KBR personnel were happy to perform the services they were there to provide. However, at the upper organizational levels, KBR is an autocratic, monolithic organization that is going to do nothing more than what the contract requires.

KBR provided on-base transportation in the form of four scheduled bus routes. They ran on very predictable schedules from about five in the morning to midnight. Three of the routes originated in the administrative area of the base. One route went to the flight line road and then to the west end of the base. One route went to the middle of the flight line area, and the third went to the east end of the flight line. The fourth route ran east/west along the flight line, connecting the other three routes.

KBR contracted to provide firefighting services for the base. One fire station served the flight line with crash recovery crews, and the other station was in the administrative area of the base to fight structural fires.

Electricity on the base came from generators serviced and maintained by KBR. The generators burned jet fuel. KBR replenished the tanks daily with a fleet of fuel trucks.

2.3 Base Amenities

The base exchange was limited but provided essentials as well as some niceties. Think of it as a 7-11 on steroids. In addition to typical 7-11 items, like chips, dips, candy, and nuts, you could get beef or chicken cups of noodles. They also carried a large selection of energy drinks from Monster and Red Bull. They didn't have any soft drinks as those were available for free in the dining facility. One aisle looked like a mini GNC with supplements for all the bodybuilders. There is no shortage of bodybuilders in the Army and Marine contingents. There was an aisle with your basic health and personal hygiene needs. Another section had cleaning supplies. The biggest area had clothing: shoes, socks, underwear, plus a large selection of T-shirts, sweatpants and shirts, and outer wear with various insignia indicating it was from an assignment at Al Asad, Operation Inherent Resolve, and Iraq. There was also a limited electronics section that had adapter plugs and 220-volt converters, as well as computers and associated hardware and gaming supplies. One thing lacking was any adult beverages since we were in a Muslim country, and we respected their cultural ban on alcohol. Prayer rugs were also available for purchase. I had no problem with the fact that we respected their culture here, but it highlighted to me that Muslims don't seem to have the same courtesy or respect for our culture and social conduct when they come to America.

The base gym was large to accommodate all the people who wanted to work out and maintain a level of fitness necessary for infantry-level combat.

The USO had two facilities on base: a main facility in the administrative area and a satellite facility in the operational area. The main facility had TV lounge areas, Ping-Pong tables, pool tables, computer gaming areas, and a telephone calling area, where you could make calls home for free. The satellite facility had a TV lounge, a Ping-Pong table, a pool table, and a computer gaming area. Free Wi-Fi was available at both locations.

A touch of home was Green Beans, a Starbucks clone. There was a walk-up facility in the operational area and a sit-down facility in the administrative area. While I was there, Subway opened a store collocated with the Green Beans facility in the administrative area.

Two companies provided WiFi service that covered the entire base so you could get online in your living quarters as well as at work or any of the dining facilities. Decent 3-megabit service cost about $130 per month, which seemed steep, but considering where we were in the middle of nowhere, it was probably reasonable. I found it certainly worth the money. Not only could you check e-mail and play games, but you could also FaceTime with family and get Netflix or Hulu, which really helped pass the time and let you stay connected with what is happening at home.

All in all, this was a small slice of Americana in the middle of the desert in Western Iraq, but in many ways, it just highlighted all the things you were missing by not being at home. A phrase associated with other remote assignments goes, "Al Asad is not the end of the world, but you can see it from here." Civilians were confined to the base for their entire time at Al Asad as it was too dangerous to venture off base in the local culture. Military personnel only went off base in armed patrols with full body armor.

Routing to Al Asad
(Photo courtesy of ForeFlight, A Boeing Company)

Al Asad Air Base
(Photo courtesy of ForeFlight, A Boeing Company)

CHUs inside T-Wall

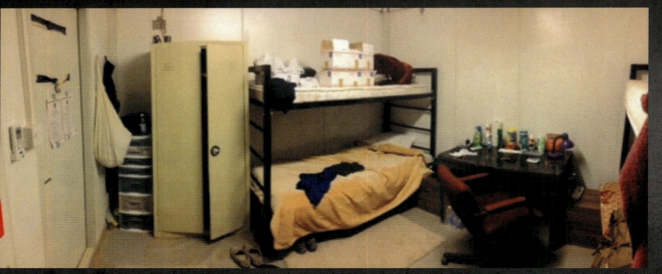

Living Quarters

Dining Facility Exterior

Dining Facility Decorated for Christmas

The Author in the Dining Facility

Base Exchange Interior

Base Exchange Exterior

Starbucks Clone

U.S. Post Office

Base Gym

Morale Lounge

Operations and Hangar Tents

French Compound

Danish Compound

Norwegian Compound

Operation Inherent Resolve Area of Responsibility (AOR)
(Photo courtesy of ForeFlight, A Boeing Company)

CHAPTER 3

Fall 2018

OPERATION INHERENT RESOLVE [1]

mercenary
noun
mer·ce·nary | \ˈmər-sə-ˌner-ē, -ne-rē\
plural **mercenaries**
Definition of *mercenary*
one that serves merely for wages *especially*: a soldier hired into foreign service

I don't think any of us met the precise definition of a mercenary for two reasons. First, no one I knew was motivated purely by the money, although we appreciated being reasonably compensated for the skills we brought to the fight. Maybe more importantly, while we were on foreign soil, we were working for US national interests rather than a foreign service. I have to say, though, I liked the sound of mercenary almost as much as I liked being called a Yankee air pirate by the North Vietnamese.

Our military calls the efforts in Iraq and Syria Operation Inherent Resolve. An unclassified description from Wikipedia provides the following overview[2]:

Operation Inherent Resolve (OIR) is the US military's operational name for the military intervention against the Islamic State of Iraq and Syria (ISIL, in the vernacular, Daesh), including both the campaign in Iraq and the campaign in Syria. Since 21 August 2016, the US Army's XVIII Airborne Corps has been responsible for Combined Joint Task Force – Operation Inherent Resolve (CJTF-OIR).

According to the military website,[1] seventy-two nations contribute to Operation Inherent Resolve in one form or another. Al Asad is strategically located in Western Iraq, which allows quick access to all areas of Iraq and Syria. US forces at Al Asad included Army, Marine, and Air Force contingents.

A consortium of Yugoslavian companies originally built Al Asad for Saddam Hussein and the Iraqi Air Force between 1981 and 1997. Then it was called Qadisiyah Air Base. American forces renamed the base Al Asad (The Lion) after Desert Storm.[2]

Army and Marine ground forces provided base security. Additionally, Air Force security police provided flight line security. I felt no trepidation being here in the fall of 2018. Two indicators let you feel at ease. Throughout the military, each base assesses the risk of the environment and assigns a Force Protection Condition. The levels start at Normal then then range from Alpha to Delta, with Alpha indicating the least threat and Delta indicating the greatest threat. The following definitions are from a US Army website[3]:

- Normal – occurs when a general global threat of possible terrorist activity is possible; the minimum FPCON for US Army commands is normal.
- Alpha – occurs when there is an increased general threat of possible terrorist activity against personnel or facilities; the nature and extent of the threat are unpredictable.
- Bravo – applies when an increased or more predictable threat of terrorist activity exists.
- Charlie – applies when an incident occurs or intelligence is received indicating some form of terrorist action or targeting against personnel or facilities is likely.;100 percent ID card check required.
- Delta – applies in the immediate area where a terrorist attack has occurred or when intelligence has been received that terrorist action against a specific location or person is imminent; 100 percent ID card check required.

The force protection level was Charlie while I was at Al Asad. Still, I was comfortable.

Additionally, the base dictates a personal protective equipment (PPE) level indicating how accessible your helmet and flak vest should be.[4] This was the same situation I encountered when I spent a week at Ben Hoa Air Base outside of Saigon in 1972, where rocket attacks were more likely to occur than any anticipated attack at Al Asad.

I may have had a different threshold for concern than people who hadn't previously been in a combat situation, but none of the other people on our team seemed particularly stressed over the situation either.

That's not to say there wasn't a threat outside the perimeter. The base did come under rocket attack in January 2020.[5] Military.com reported that there were no fatalities, but approximately one hundred military were injured.[6] Looking at the poststrike photos, I could see where the rockets hit in relation to my quarters and our ops area. Neither area was damaged in the attack.

General Atomics contracts with the Air Force to provide pilots and sensor operators to fly Air Force MQ-9s on Intelligence, Surveillance and Reconnaissance (ISR) missions to support Operation Inherent Resolve from Al Asad.[7] The operation is called a GOCO, which stands for Government Owned, Contractor Operated organization. The Geneva Convention prohibits civilians (contractors) from being involved in any weapons deliveries.

We did surveillance and reconnaissance missions throughout the Inherent Resolve operational area. Our missions were seventeen to eighteen hours long.[30] Once we got airborne, we received our tasking from our command and control element through a secure communications channel.

Unlike my experience in Vietnam, every bomb I observed had a specific target. Each bomb was a precision-guided weapon, so it struck exactly where the targeting cell wanted it.

In Vietnam, if the weather was too bad to work targets visually with our unguided weapons, we would frequently be told to fly a heading and altitude over a known enemy area, ripple-drop all twelve bombs on each aircraft into the clouds based on a direction and range from a known location. All we were certain of was that they would hit the ground. We just hoped there was something worth bombing there. We called this killing suspected enemy trees. On more than one occasion at night, I was able to observe secondary explosions after the bombs went off, meaning we actually hit a target worth bombing.

On a twelve-hour shift, I would spend three to six hours in the control van flying the drone to the location the sensor operator needed to be to monitor the specified target. Sometimes that was broken up into smaller segments, but at other times it was a straight six hours in the chair. In my mind, my job was the easier of the two. I could use the autopilot to program an orbit around the target, and all I had to do was monitor the aircraft to make sure it was doing what I programmed and all systems were functioning normally. The sensor operator was busy all the time selecting the best video source and then working to get the best image by controlling the zoom and exposure settings.

Our local area orientation and in-briefing were disappointing. It was nonexistent compared with what I was used to when deploying or moving to a new base in the Air Force. When I was on active duty, there was a checklist for the things we needed to do and briefings we should get. In Al Asad, except for some specific things we needed to do, check in was a paper drill. The most detailed activity was to get the necessary badges to access classified and unclassified computers.

Before you went to the office where these badges were issued, you had to visit another office to review and approve the authorization for the badge. These were black-and-white items on the in-processing checklist that had to be done. Another item on the checklist was a briefing on the special instructions (SPINs). The SPINs are voluminous, and for any given mission, there's only a small part of the SPINs that apply to your flight. In the Air Force when you deployed, a person familiar with the operation and SPINs would brief you on the parts of the SPINs that applied to what you were doing and explain them in English rather than military speak. The briefing for us at Al Asad was simply to show us how to find the SPINs document on the classified network, and we were left to our own to try to sort through them to find sections that applied to unmanned verses manned aircraft operations for each of the areas where we would be flying.

3.2 A Flight

In preparation for a flight from Al Asad, the launch pilot would confirm the flight's tasking and check the weather. In the Air Force, I was an aircraft commander, flight leader, mission commander, and supervisor of flying, making go/no-go decisions for twenty-one years. It was nice to be able to sit back and let the launch pilot worry about those details. After getting the initial tasking and weather, the launch pilot and sensor operator leave the ready room to preflight the aircraft and then go to the control van to start the launch process. This involves making sure the van and aircraft are set to the correct frequencies followed by start, taxi, and takeoff. Normal VHF radios are used to communicate with ground control and the tower for taxi and takeoff. Prior to taxiing, the launch pilot will contact the airspace coordinator to get an assigned altitude for the mission. Shortly after takeoff, the launch crew will transition the drone and control van from the line-of-sight launch frequencies to the over-the-horizon satellite frequencies. There are two options for getting to the altitude you will be using: The best option is to be cleared to climb to altitude en route to your working, airspace which happens frequently if there's no conflicting traffic between the airport and the assigned airspace. The other option is to be sent to a specific area to climb in place until you get to your working altitude and then being cleared to your working area. The military airspace controller will coordinate with civilian air traffic controllers to deconflict military and civilian traffic.

Out of necessity, air traffic control in the OIR airspace for blending manned and unmanned aircraft, military and civilian, is far more advanced than air traffic control in the United States. It's a great demonstration platform that could be used to help US air traffic control develop procedures and confidence to integrate unmanned aircraft into the national airspace system in the United States.

Somewhere en route, the mission pilot and mission sensor operator will relieve the launch crew. While the capability exists for the mission crew to be in a different control van back in the United States, at Al Asad, it was simply a matter of the launch crew getting out of their seats in the van and the mission crew sitting down to continue the flight. The question of why our contract has the mission crews colocated with the launch-and-recovery crews at Al Asad rather than somewhere in the States is a mystery to me. One possibility is that it kept the contract administration and accounting neatly discrete, so the Air Force knew the assigned manpower to accomplish the mission was dedicated to that contract and not doing anything else. Another explanation is that if you use remote operations, you need two control vans: one van at the operational base to launch and recover the aircraft and another van in the remote location to control the aircraft during the mission. The way we operated, there was only one van needed per flight.

After I flew to the area, as pilot, I would set up an orbit over the designated area of interest, then the sensor operator would look at specific areas or buildings as directed by the operational controller. Sometimes the task is to simply monitor a building, looking for people coming to and going from the building. Other times we would be told to look at a target so the scanner could determine there were no civilians present prior to a strike and then to capture images of the strike and poststrike to assess the effectiveness of the strike.

Since we were flying seventeen- and eighteen-hour missions,[30] the mission pilots and sensors would take turns in the control van, and in every case, each mission would flow from night shift to day shift or the other way around. Over the duration of the mission, the points of interest would change and the pilot would need to reposition the orbit to put the aircraft in a good position for the sensor operator to monitor the assigned target.

At the end of the tasked on-station time, the mission crew would coordinate a return to Al Asad then start heading home. Somewhere on the way home, the recovery crew would take over from the mission crew and land the aircraft.

Once the crew shut the aircraft down the ground, crews had about six hours to get the airplane ready for the next flight. Our aircraft were extremely reliable, so we rarely had any problems being ready for the next flight. We generally had three aircraft flying with staggered takeoff and landing times.

The interactions of the members of the deployed personnel are not at all like the cohesiveness of a fighter squadron. Because of the short three-month duration of deployments, individuals come and go on a weekly basis, unlike fighter squadrons where assignments are usually for three years. In a fighter squadron, each of us bonded and functioned as a team. Everybody took care of his wingman and leader. Flying drones, you are in the control van with a sensor operator for maybe two hours before one of you changes out. Worse, you don't both change out at the same time, so there is a lost element of crew integrity that carries over into the ready room. In the ready room, people are on headsets playing games, video-chatting, taking care of e-mails, and updating their Facebook page. One aspect that struck me was the fact that at mealtime, people on a shift tended to go the dining facility, get their meal in a box, and take it back to the ready room to eat. I much preferred to go to the dining facility, have a relaxing sit-down meal, and then go back to the ready room. That's not to say there wasn't a common sense of purpose and helping one another, but it just wasn't the same. In a fighter squadron, when you were deployed, we did everything as a group. We had a great time.

remember one deployment to Norway, where we went to a squadron dinner at a nice restaurant on the weekend. The squadron operations officer was the deployment commander. He was notorious for getting one bill for the group and dividing the amount by the number of people in the group to determine how much each should pay with a tip thrown in. His trick was to always order the most expensive items on the menu and let everyone else help pay for his high living. Our group of deployed pilots was on to this, so we colluded to do the same thing and really enjoy ourselves. This was in the early 1980s, and the bill for the ten of us was close to $1,500. He learned we were on to his game. It was a great evening! On another deployment to Italy, we went to dinner at one of our favorite restaurants on a hill overlooking the city of Cagliari on the island of Sardinia. While we were eating, pilots from a Canadian F-18 squadron showed up to have dinner there as well. We started taking turns singing fighter pilot songs to each other. We would sing a song for them, and then they would sing a song for us. We were singing in English, thinking the locals wouldn't understand the words. Fighter pilot songs have never been politically correct by any standards, today or yesteryear. When the Carabinieri, federal police, showed up en force, we decided it was time to pay the bill and leave.

There was no comparable comradery at the deployed drone locations. Part of it may have been the fact there was no place to go, and another contributor may have been the twelve-on-twelve-off shifts, but I don't think that was the major reason. My generational gap with the majority of the deployed pilots and sensors may also have been a factor, but I don't have any trouble having a good time at parties and dinners with my sons and their friends.

3.3 A Day in the Life

If working twelve hours a day, seven days a week, sounds grueling, it is. On the other hand, the pace is slow and tedious. It took me about a month to slow down and get into a rhythm and pace. Additionally, having a day off would be really boring as there's no place to go and no real activities to take part in. Besides, you're only making money when you are working. Better to be doing that than doing nothing. Being on the night shift, I would get off work between three and four in the morning and walk three-quarters of a mile from the ops tent to my CHU. I would unwind for about half an hour and then go to bed. One thing I appreciated about the night shift was that I could sleep in and get up when I felt like it rather than needing to set an alarm to get ready to go to work like the day shift; they had to be at work at four in the morning. I would wake up around noon, shower, and head to lunch.

After lunch, I would walk a mile to the base exchange and back for a "shelf-check." There was usually nothing I needed or anything new to see, but it was a good excuse for a walk. A base exchange shelf-check was always something we would do when we deployed in the Air Force. After I got back to the CHU, I would check e-mails and Facebook, usually not much activity because it was still the middle of the night back in the States. I left the CHU for a mile walk to work around three in the afternoon, arriving at the ops tent in time for the 4:00 p.m. shift-change.

Once I dropped off my backpack and checked e-mail at work, I would leave the ops ready room for another mile walk on a different route to the base exchange to verify that nothing on the shelves had changed since my visit a few hours earlier. Then it was a mile walk to dinner and back to the ready room to fly my scheduled time or times. Somewhere between 11:00 p.m. and 1:00 a.m., I would get a break for midnight dinner. If it was a short break between times in the control van, I would take the company truck to the dining facility to get a takeout box, but if I had time, I would walk the three-quarter mile to the dining facility for a sit-down meal and break from work. In all, I was walking about six miles a day.

During breaks, I could keep up with Facebook posts and e-mail family and friends since it was now daytime back in the States. On weekends, I would FaceTime with my two boys and their families.

Then it was off to the CHU, between 3:00 a.m. and 4:00 a.m., to be ready to repeat the process again. I felt like Bill Murray in the movie *Ground Hog Day*. Do this for ninety days and it's time to go home.

While I only saw my roommate in passing during shift-change, he was still a catastrophe to live with. I'm no Felix Unger from the movie *The Odd Couple*, but my roommate would give Oscar Madison a run for the money. His side of the room always looked like the aftermath of an earthquake, with clothes spilling out of his locker, a bed that was never made, and things strewn on the floor. He drove people crazy during training in California as he was always wound up tighter than a drum, talked incessantly and always at three hundred words a minute. He didn't slow down on deployment in Iraq, so it was

There was nothing worth getting stressed out about for our operations. It seemed that any stress people felt was self-imposed based on a desire to do well and not screw up. This, in my mind, is because we weren't dropping weapons and striking targets, which is where military drone pilots can suffer from real-time stress and post-traumatic stress disorder (PTSD). They could easily suffer greatly if they missed a target, killed some civilians, or inadvertently struck a friendly position. Though rare, that happened. The pilots and sensor operators had to deal with having clearly seen the results of their mistakes—our images were superb. I was on a flight in South Vietnam, where another person in the flight did not program his weapons release computer properly and missed the intended target by about a mile. Fortunately, there were no civilian casualties, but it's a burden he's lived with ever since. In this job, it's something we all live with. A commander of a drone unit I know had one of his pilots bomb and kill friendly troops based on a misidentification by the forward air controller in Afghanistan while he was flying the drone from a location in the United States. The pilot took it very hard, and the commander had to have people monitor him to prevent the pilot's suicide.

Veteran-manned pilots I know sometimes joke about drone pilots flying "combat" sitting in the safety of a control van miles or half a world away from any threats. One commander I spoke with in Las Vegas said it was, in fact, a strange feeling to have breakfast with your wife and children, drive to work, get in the van, fly a combat mission, bomb targets, and then go home to a nice dinner and help the kids with their homework. Having flown my share of combat missions, where I did get shot at by missiles and artillery, I was not the least bit embarrassed or apologetic about sitting in the comfort of a van knowing if the drone did get shot down, I could get up, walk out of the van, go back to the CHU, and get a good night's sleep while the Air Force found another drone for me to fly.

3.4 Questions

Were we doing any good? Absolutely! The efforts of Operation Inherent Resolve effectively denied ISIS any real offensive capability in the region or the rest of the world. We put the bully at bay. Al Asad, Ramadi, and Fallujah have been taken out of ISIS control, and ISIS-controlled territory has been limited to a small area in Eastern Syria near the border of Iraq. Our success is the reason it was safe to be there as demonstrated by President Trump's visit to Al Asad while I was there. Unfortunately, I was in the van flying a mission the whole time he was on the ground. It wouldn't have mattered because this was a show of support for our military. They only wanted people in uniform in the photo ops, so contractors were not invited to any of his appearances while he and Melania visited the base.

A different question, though, is, *are we winning?* I don't think we have a true vision or definition of what winning is. There is no head of state or government representative with whom to sign a surrender or end the conflict. We are trying to provide an environment in which the country can try to develop a representative government, but I'm not sure the people here know what that is or even if it's worth their effort to fight for. We can't force it on them. It must come from within, and for that to happen, centuries of tradition, culture, dogma, and inertia need to change on an individual rather than a national level. People flee countries ruled by Islamic majorities to avoid the oppression that comes with Sharia Law. Yet when they get to a country that looks attractive to them, which isn't a Muslim-majority country, one of the first things many do is start trying to recreate a culture, like the one from which they fled, to include Sharia Law. In countries where Muslims are in the minority, they clamor for minority rights, yet in countries where Muslims are in the majority, minority rights are trampled.

Many Westerners naïvely project our beliefs and culture on everyone we meet. We think if we treat people with dignity and respect, they will reciprocate. That simply isn't true, no matter how much we would like it to be. While assigned to the Red Flag planning staff at Nellis AFB, Nevada, I had the opportunity to attend Soviet awareness school at Air Force headquarters on Bolling AFB. We learned that communist governments have absolutely no problem in dealings with others to smile, nod, and say what the person they are dealing with wants to hear while pursuing their interests, even if they aren't what they said or promised to do. Putin's actions in the Ukraine over the years are a good example, and he's trying to rewrite history according to his perceptions. Extreme Muslims also have no problem lying to infidels to accomplish their true goals. To be sure, there are Christians who are equally as fervent and radical as some Muslims, but there are a good many Christians who believe everybody can live in harmony, regardless of their religious background. I don't think that is the case for Islam, particularly radical Muslims. In many verses, the Quran teaches that all must succumb to Islam or be killed. There is no middle ground that allows for differing religious beliefs to peacefully coexist. Unlike President Bush 43 at the site of the World Trade Center after it was attacked, I won't liken our current efforts to the crusades. I don't think Christians are out to convert all Muslims to Christianity; they are just seeking an elusive solution where people of different faiths and backgrounds can get along amicably. I do think the radical followers of Mohammed have never stopped fighting the crusades. The tenacity of Osama bin Laden, in his efforts to destroy the World Trade Center over decades, is a prime modern example of Islamic resolve versus the short span of attention Westerners have.

What happens if we just give up on the situation and pull out? Even if other Western nations might understand we gave it our best effort, our credibility with governments in the Middle East would be irreparably damaged. More importantly, the conditions that spawned ISIS, the Taliban, and Al-Qaeda would foster these or similar movements that would continue to be a threat to world peace and Western civilizations. It's a quagmire that can't be ignored, and I don't see a ready solution.

In my mind, the disastrous results of our hasty withdrawal from Afghanistan in the fall of 2021 validate my perceptions gained at Al Asad in 2018.

CHAPTER 4

Summer 2019

INTO AFRICA

Leaving Al Asad, the plan was for me to return in three months, but the only thing constant in military operations is change. Once I got back to San Diego, I learned that our operations at Al Asad were cancelled, and I would now have a five-month break before deploying to Niamey, Niger, in July 2019. The extra time at home was just fine to me, even though it meant that the deployment to Africa starting in July and ending in September would be my only deployment for this year. The company normally tries, successfully, to make sure their deploying aircrews get six months of deployment every year, so you make enough money each year to have a decent income. That was not an issue for me. With my other incomes, I didn't need to work that much anymore. A big plus to me was the fact that I would now be on a rotation schedule that would allow me to be at home for Thanksgiving and Christmas.

The first thing I did was check the State Department's website for information on Niger and found that they advised against travel to Niger because of the volatile political environment, civil unrest, and the potential for kidnappings. One of the pilots who went through training with me at GA-ASI's flight operations facility was currently deployed to Niamey, and I e-mailed him for information on the site. I learned that while the base of operation was located on the international airport that serves Niamey, the capital of Niger, the living conditions on base were more primitive than the facilities at Al Asad. In Al Asad, we lived in prefabricated trailers. In Niamey, everyone lived in tents. Each tent has eight small rooms made with plywood walls and just enough space for a bed. The base itself is much smaller than Al Asad and confined to the northwest corner of the international airport at Niamey.

The deployment support team is located at the General Atomics facilities in the San Diego area. Since aircrews can live anywhere in the United States when they are not deployed, the primary ways to interact with the deployment coordinators are e-mail and telephone. I was able to work with them in person and enjoyed getting to know them and letting them put a face with my name. This team does an excellent job not only coordinating all travel for deploying aircrews, but they also take care of getting our travel expense reports entered into the not-too-user-friendly travel expense system at General Atomics. Having aircrews complete their travel expense reports actually created more problems correcting mistakes than having people who understood the system taking our information from a simple form that listed all our travel and expenses and then entering the information into the system required by the people who tracked and paid the expenses. The pre-deployment process began three months before my deployment date. It included renewing training in several online courses to meet military training requirements, getting a pre-deployment physical and dental exam, making sure I had all the required immunizations, including yellow fever, and getting the required visa from the Niger Embassy in Washington DC.

Aircrew members also must have recent experience flying, called currency, to be able to conduct a flight. For me, to be able to fly without the supervision of an instructor pilot, the requirement is to have flown a flight in the previous forty-five days. With more than four months of not flying, it meant a trip back to GA-ASI's flight operations facility to fly with an instructor and finish up all the administrative checklists. My trip to GA-ASI's flight operations facility was scheduled for the first two weeks in June. When I got to GA-ASI's flight operations facility, I was pleasantly surprised to find that scheduling and training was a lot more organized and efficient than when I was there for my initial training. I was able to get everything done in a week and a half and go home two days earlier than planned. While I was at GA-ASI's flight operations facility, I established e-mail communication with the pilot I would be replacing, who gave me some good suggestions of things to bring that I would not have thought of. Most important was the fact that even though the daytime temperatures were in the triple digits and the nighttime temperatures were in the upper eighties, the tents get very cold at night because of the air conditioning, so you need something for a quilt or heavy blanket to be comfortable. The recommendation was a lightweight sleeping bag that could be unzipped and used as a top cover.

Travel to Niamey was straightforward: San Diego to Salt Lake City with a four-hour layover to connect with an overnight Delta flight to Paris, arriving midmorning with a reservation at the hotel located on the airport, and then a direct flight to Niamey on Air France the next morning. After the five-hour flight to Niamey, the site lead was waiting for me at the terminal on the south side of the airport, and then it was a quick drive to the military installation on the north side of the airport.[7] Several countries, including French, Canadians, Germans, and Italians, in addition to the Americans, have military personnel assigned there, and each country has a separate compound within the post perimeter.

The American compound is officially known as Air Base 101. The Americans here are called an Early Response Force (ERF), but in fact, it is a long-term activity. Signage around the facility indicated it was built by Navy Seabees in early 2015.

Our first stop was the American operational area. When we drove up, there was a big barbecue party going on, with hamburgers and small steaks, since weather in the operational area was bad, and there was no flying that day. I knew right away that this was going to be a more enjoyable working environment. There were several people there who went through initial training at the same time I did, so it was nice to see familiar faces, and they were happy to see me. After meeting everyone and having some of the BBQ, I got my room assignment and learned that my working shift would be from two in the afternoon to two in the morning, which was just what I wanted. Next, we headed to the American administrative compound about a mile from the ops area.

The admin area has all the support facilities in addition to the housing tents. Those facilities include the dining facility tent, the morale and welfare USO tent, the post office, the chapel, the clinic, the do-it-yourself laundromat, and the base exchange.

Unlike Al Asad, all support activities, like billeting and messing, are run by the Air Force. There was no contracted support from KBR.

I was prepared for a small bare-bones room, but it was worse than I imagined. The only thing in the "room" was a bed. No locker, no dresser, no other furniture whatsoever. The bad news was that I would have to build any furniture I wanted. The good news(?) was that they had all the lumber and plywood I would need. In addition, since people on both shifts are in the same tents, the tents are dark, and it's quiet hours 24/7. You need a flashlight to negotiate the hallway, and you use a small electric lantern that you bring with you, so light doesn't spill into your neighbors' rooms. I couldn't unpack my bag because there was no place to put my clothes, so I went to dinner at the dining tent. When I got back to my tent, the first thing I did was make my bed with the bedding I brought with me. Once I got that done, I was ready to go to bed.

Just like Al Asad, the latrine and shower facilities are communal. Those nearest my tent were about fifty yards away. I was smart enough to realize that getting up in the middle of the night to go to the bathroom, particularly during monsoon season, would be a pain, so I brought a pee jar, and that proved to be brilliant.

Strangely enough, even though the conditions here are more austere than at Al Asad, the pay bump is less than at Al Asad because this is not a combat zone.

Communications locally and back home were very convenient and well organized, thanks to WiFi, the Internet, and various cell phone applications. Anytime I was in WiFi coverage, I had WiFi calling available on my phone. That meant I could dial any stateside telephone number and be connected with no long distance or roaming fees. Also, people in the States could call my number and have no idea I was in Africa. FaceTime worked just fine too, so I was able to see and talk to family when our schedules meshed. Locally, we used WhatsApp to communicate and had several user groups on that for various functions. We had an aircrew back channel, where we could coordinate activities, such as trips between the admin area and ops or going downtown for dinner, poke fun at one another, or make general snarky comments, if we wanted to vent. For people who have been in an Air Force flying squadron, this was the equivalent of the Duffer Book.

It had been a month since my currency flight at GA-ASI's flight operations facility, so I was eager to fly to be able to update my currency before my forty-five days expired. That first afternoon I met the crew van at the designated pickup point and headed to work. The lead pilot also wanted me to fly as soon as possible before the monsoons started, so after taking care of some necessary paperwork and reviewing the rules for flying, here I went in the box to fly with over-the-shoulder help from the pilot I was replacing. I flew a total of five hours that day and got familiar with the operational procedures and the rules for our working area.

Two days later, the weather was again poor, so I had the opportunity to build a nightstand to go next to the bed. That exercised some new muscles. I was tired and sore when I got done building the two-tiered nightstand with one level at the same height as the bed and another level above that. That helped a little as I could put my carry-on bag under the nightstand, but I was still tripping over my suitcase on the floor with all my clothes in it. The prospect of living out of my suitcase for the next three months was ugly. Two nights later, I was able to build a three-tiered shelf, and that made a vast improvement. I was able to unpack all my clothes and put my big suitcase out of the way under my bed. Suddenly, the room became much more livable.

After my experience at Al Asad, I was able to adjust more quickly to the slower pace of life and fall into a routine. The thing I liked about being on the night schedule was that again I went to bed right after I got off work, usually before 2:00 a.m., and then slept until I felt like getting up, again without the use of an alarm clock, normally around 9:00 a.m. or 10:00 a.m. I would get ready for the day, get dressed, and go to the midday meal at eleven. After lunch, around noon, I went to the Morale, Welfare and Recreation (MWR) tent to check e-mail, Facebook, Instagram, and instant messages using an app called Signal. At one o'clock, I had the option to go to the pickup point to catch the crew van to work or walk. Initially, I rode the crew van, but after I acclimated to the heat, I preferred to walk and get some exercise. I was usually first in the box on our shift and flew from two to five thirty and then went to dinner. If our vulnerability time ended before midnight, that's the only flying I did. If we flew after midnight, I'd spend another hour or two flying for a second period before starting the return to base and turning over the seat to the landing pilot.

A big difference between Niamey and Al Asad was that we were able to go off base and into Niamey when the flying schedule allowed. That made for pleasant breaks away from the austerity of the base. There were shops and restaurants that were very enjoyable and a treat anytime we could get away. A noticeable difference between the restaurants in Niamey and in the States, however, was the fact that each was a gated compound with armed guards, but once inside, they were a breath of fresh air, with distinctive decors and food that was much better than what we got at the dining facility on base. One nice thing about the contracted KBR dining facilities at Al Asad was the fact that certain days had a known menu. Wednesdays were pizza day, Friday was crab dinner, Sunday was roast beef. They also had special days like Mongolian barbeque. That was not the case at Niamey. There was no apparent schedule for certain meals, usually two nondescript meats, instant mashed potatoes, pasta or rice, and mushy canned vegetables.

There were other noticeable differences. Since the base in Africa was much smaller, you were able to recognize people in different groups, and there just seemed to be more cohesion and sense of community. There was a gate into and out of the operations area as well as a gate into and out of the administrative/residential area. Both were attended by Air Force security police, whose faces we came to know and could recognize in the dining facility. The security personnel also learned our faces. Occasionally, one of us would forget our ID badge. The guard would recognize that person with the rest of us and let that person in with us. In Al Asad, the post office was run by the Army. They were very cold in dealing with customers, almost as if you were interrupting their day. They only operated for three hours a day on Monday, Wednesday, and Friday. On the other hand, the post office at Niamey was run by the Air Force. They were open Monday through Friday, from 8:00 a.m. to 5:00 p.m., and Saturday, from 8:00 a.m. to 1:00 p.m. The people running the post office were friendly and happy to help customers. The base exchange at Al Asad was a little larger than a 7/11 and was open seven days a week, from 9:00 a.m. to 9:00 p.m., with a dedicated staff. At Niamey, the base exchange was a twenty-by-twenty-foot room with very limited stock. It was usually open Monday, Wednesday, and Friday, from eleven thirty to one and then again from three to five. The people who ran the MWR tent did double duty and staffed the exchange when it was open.

Open-source information on drone operations in Africa can be found on the Internet. According to an online release by the Voice of America:

The US started operating (unarmed Intelligence, Surveillance and Reconnaissance) ISR drones in Niamey in 2013 in support of French military operations in neighboring Mali and 'other regional requirements' according to the US Air Force. [12]

Other articles on the Internet indicate that armed drones were deployed to Niamey in 2017 after four American military personnel were ambushed and killed conducting operations in Niger. [13]

As in Iraq, my job was to fly unarmed ISR drones to locate insurgents and terrorists in our area of operation and support French and Niger forces. Armed drones can only be flown by military personnel as mandated by the Geneva Convention. The French Air Force operated armed MQ-9s and manned Mirage fighter aircraft at Niamey.

Airspace coordination was much simpler in Africa than Iraq since there was so much less military traffic to contend with. As in Iraq, we would send our airspace request to a central American coordinator who would then work with the civilian air traffic control system to get approval to operate in our requested area. In Iraq, we would request an altitude and an area that was a box thirty-by-thirty miles. In Africa, we did the same, but the box was ninety-by-ninety miles. In Iraq, we were operating from a military air base that was predominately a drone base but also had manned military aircraft operations. In Africa, we operated from a civilian international airport that had commercial airliners using the same runway. Unlike the FAA in the United States, the local controllers have adapted to this mode of operation, and they procedurally separate manned and unmanned aircraft operating in and out of the airport.

The major operational concern in Africa was the weather, particularly during the monsoon season. Understandably, you look at the forecast for the airfield for your departure, the target area, and the return to the airfield fourteen to sixteen hours later. There are no alternates as you must land at the same place where you took off. Once you are airborne, you continue to monitor the weather at home base for any un-forecast surprises, realizing you can be as much as two or four hours from home. Additionally, you must monitor the weather between home base and your working area to watch for weather that could cut you off and prevent getting back to your home base. This falls on the pilot as the sensor operator is busy focusing the cameras on the targets he or she has been told to monitor. In the control van, you have various resources to monitor current weather and watch developing weather. An aviation application available to all civilian general aviation pilots is called ForeFlight. In addition to providing flight-planning software, it can display current satellite and weather radar imagery anywhere in the world. Military software uses the same satellite imagery to produce different displays of that information. The pilot also has a direct line to military forecasters anytime there's a question or an update is desired. During the monsoon season, cells of thunderstorms can develop rapidly. More than once, we aborted a mission early because of the developing weather at home base or between the target area and home, and I dodged billowing cumulus buildups to get home. Once you are in a weather abort situation, the sensor operator then uses all his cameras to help the pilot avoid bad weather. The pilot has additional help monitoring the weather from the operations supervisor who keeps an eye on the weather in the ready room as well. Another technique when you have stable weather that can be forecast is to overfly bad weather. This involves taking off in good weather when bad weather is forecast for the home field while you are airborne but predicted to be good again when you are scheduled to land as long as the bad weather won't get between you and the airfield when it's time to recover. I did not like doing this. You are relying on the forecast to be accurate. It's like trying to draw to an inside straight in poker.

Routing to Niamey
(Photo courtesy of ForeFlight, A Boeing Company)

Niamey International Airport
(Photo courtesy of ForeFlight, A Boeing Company)

African Area of Operations (Google Maps)

Monsoon Weather
(Photo courtesy of ForeFlight, A Boeing Company)

Haboob at the Base

Sleeping Quarters

Living Quarters

Base Exchange

Saturday Bazaar at Front Gate

Enjoying Local Culture

French Restaurant

Outdoor Gated Restaurant

CHAPTER 5

Fall 2020

THE IRON CURTAIN

During the Cold War, democratic nations of Western Europe, Canada, and the United States were pitted against the totalitarian communist regimes of Eastern Europe. The geographical borders between those two blocks were frequently referred to as the Iron Curtain because of the closed nature of the countries under the influence of the Soviet Union.

The Western nations were unified by the North Atlantic Treaty Organization (NATO), but each was a sovereign nation. The major unifying provision of NATO was the commitment by all member nations that if one nation was attacked, it would amount to an attack on all the countries in the organization and all of them would respond. This aspect of the treaty stemmed from the recent history of World War II, where Hitler invaded one country at a time while all the others watched and tried to appease him just hoping they would not be next. The twelve original countries of NATO included Belgium, Britain, Canada, Denmark, France, Iceland, Italy, Luxembourg, the Netherlands, Norway, Portugal, and the United States.

The nations east of the Iron Curtain were an amalgamation of the Union of Soviet Socialist Republics (USSR) called the Soviet Union and the Warsaw Pact. The fifteen republics of the Soviet Union included Russia, Ukraine, Georgia, Belorussia, Uzbekistan, Armenia, Azerbaijan, Kazakhstan, Kyrgyzstan, Moldova, Turkmenistan, Tajikistan, Latvia, Lithuania, and Estonia. The eastern counterpart of NATO was the Warsaw Pact consisting of the USSR, Albania, Bulgaria, Czechoslovakia, East Germany, Hungary, Poland, and Romania. While all claimed to be sovereign nations on paper, the fact of the matter was they were all tightly controlled and dominated by Russia from Moscow. Warsaw Pact nations had their own standing military, but they were all subservient to the Russian military forces occupying ch countries. The stated purpose of the Warsaw Pact countries was to counter the NATO countries. In reality, they were simply a buffer for Russia to protect the Motherland.

My four Air Force assignments in Europe occurred during the Cold War. The first was a frontline operational tour at Spangdahlem Air Base, Germany, just east of Luxemburg, where I sat nuclear alert in the F-4, from 1973 to 1976. The second assignment, from 1982 to 1985, was a staff tour at the headquarters for US Air Forces in Europe. The third assignment was another operational tour in the F-15 sitting air defense alert, from 1985 to 1987. The last assignment was on the Italian air base at Deccimomanu, Italy, from 1987 to 1989, as the deputy commander of US Air Force operations at that base, along with counterparts from the German, British, and Italian air forces.

The Cold War is generally considered to have lasted from 1947 to 1991, with the highest tensions being from 1947 to the early 1970s. In 1969, a policy of "Détente," French for easing or relaxation, moderated the Cold War and led to more productive interaction between the Western and Eastern nations of Europe, the United States, and Canada. This was followed by a period of Perestroika, or restructuring, in the Soviet Union, beginning in 1985. The purpose of Perestroika was to transition the Soviet economy from a centrally controlled system to a more responsive approach that was sensitive to but not completely adapted to market demands. This transition is credited with ending the Cold War, the end of the Warsaw Pact, and the collapse of the USSR to more independent republics. The Berlin Wall came down in November 1989, while I was stationed in Italy.

After years of tyranny under the Soviet Union, Warsaw Pact nations and former Soviet Republics were eager to get as much political distance from Moscow as possible and solidify their independence. To that end, the countries of the Czech Republic, Hungary and Poland (1999), Bulgaria, Estonia, Latvia, Lithuania, Romania, Slovakia and Slovenia (2004), Albania and Croatia (2009), Montenegro (2017), and North Macedonia have all joined NATO to help ensure their sovereignty.[9] What once was East Germany automatically became a part of NATO when Germany was reunified.

With this background, it is easy to see why I was eager for my next deployment to fly the MQ-9 Reaper at Miroslawiec (pronounced Miro-swaw-yitz) Air Base, Poland, in the fall of 2020.[10]

Some would say that the Iron Curtain went away with the collapse of the Soviet Union and the disbanding of the Warsaw Pact. My perception is that it simply moved east to Russia's western border. The buffer zone between democratic Western nations and the totalitarian Russian rule is gone. This, in my mind, provides insight to Russian President Putin's actions and motives in places like Ukraine. It also explains why former Soviet republics and Warsaw Pact nations move slowly toward free economies. Russians are notoriously paranoid about being invaded to the point that they fear and accuse Western governments of aggression and expansionism in international and domestic forums. It is also why Putin is hard over about not wanting Ukraine to join NATO.

During the COVID pandemic, our travel coordinators and schedulers were challenged to extremes. Many countries where we had personnel halted all commercial flights into and out of the country. Pilots and maintainers were stranded and involuntarily extended at their deployed location, and the company was unable to get replacements to the deployed locations. The travel coordinators had to keep up with travel restrictions, not only in the countries where we had flight operations, but also in any countries personnel had to pass through to get to their destinations. The personnel schedulers were forced to reflow deployment schedules often because of travel restrictions and changing quarantine requirements. My schedule was changed several times as deployments changed from the normal ninety-day deployment to a 105-day deployment to allow for quarantine after arrival at the deployed site.

Getting to Miroslawiec was challenging during the COVID pandemic. I had two letters in my possession, one from my company and one from the Department of Defense, saying I was a mission essential, critical asset allowed to travel during the pandemic.

My routing to Miroslawiec was from San Diego to Los Angeles and then to Berlin via Frankfurt by air. From Berlin, it was a three-hour drive to the town where the base is located. When I checked in for my flights at Lindbergh Field in San Diego, the ticket agent said he could not issue the boarding passes because Germany was not allowing Americans to enter the country. I pulled out my letters and gave them to the agent. He read the letters, called his boss, had an animated discussion, returned the letters, and handed me my boarding passes for the three flights. Twenty-two hours later, I was at Tegel Airport, northwest of Berlin, looking for an Uber ride to the Hilton in Central Berlin. The last time I was in Berlin, it was a divided city, and the passage from West Berlin to East Berlin was Checkpoint Charlie, which is still there as a historical point of interest. Checkpoint Charlie was a short walk from the Hilton, so I took the opportunity to revisit that location.

Having lived in Germany off and on for seven years, I knew I could handle the drive from Berlin to the base, but I was not looking forward to negotiating traffic in Berlin. Fortunately, the company was able to send a car and driver to get me and another person to our new assignment.

Once out of Berlin, the German countryside was very familiar, and it was fun to be on an Autobahn again. Driving through the farmland, I could smell the freshly plowed fields. Much to my dismay, the border between Germany and Poland was a nonevent for two reasons. During the Cold War, East Germany and Poland were allies in the Warsaw Pact. Today Germany and Poland are members of the European Union, and the borders between EU members are open.

The village of Miroslawiec was a private town in European feudal days, meaning it was owned by a local land baron and the inhabitants were subjects who worked the land and provided services to the residents. Today it is predominantly a farming community with about five thousand residents. In addition to the farms, there are also some small domesticated bison herds and a national park nearby.[11]

The 12th Air Base of the Polish Air Force is located three miles north of the village.[11]

Up until a week before I arrived, the Polish government was requiring visitors to Poland to quarantine for fourteen days before visiting or doing any business in Poland. That requirement was reduced to seven days and a negative COVID test the week before I got there. Our flats were spartan by American standards but luxurious compared with the living quarters in Iraq and Niger. Each flat was designed with two or three bedrooms, a small living room, and a kitchen. Two flats were dedicated for use by new arrivals to quarantine in, after which you were moved to your permanent flat for the rest of your four-month deployment. Oddly enough, the buildings were very similar to the military housing areas on the American bases in Germany. They were four and five stories tall with no elevators. My flat was on the fourth floor. Climbing the stairs, leaving and returning to my apartment, I often thought of Penny, Sheldon, and Leonard in the TV show *The Big Bang Theory*.

The pilot I was replacing was understandably happy for my arrival. He made a provisioning run to the local grocery store just before my arrival and was at the quarantine flat when the other new guy and I arrived. The pilot I was replacing and the company site leader made sure we understood we were not to leave the flat during our seven-day quarantine and let us know they would make other supply runs for us while we were in quarantine, we just had to ask.

The American unit flying the drones at the Polish air base is Detachment 2 of the 52nd Expeditionary Operations Group (52nd EOG), a subordinate unit of the 52nd Tactical Fighter Wing (52nd TFW), located at Spangdahlem Air Base, Germany.[10] My first assignment in Germany was flying F-4s with the 23rd Tactical Fighter Squadron of the 52nd TFW at Spangdahlem, from July 1973 to January 1976. So forty-four years later, I was once again assigned to the 52nd TFW, this time as a civilian contractor.

As in Africa, communications were easy because of WiFi and the Internet, with WiFi calling and FaceTime available for calling friends and family in the States. Locally, we used an app called Signal, like WhatsApp, with several discrete groups for various communications. There was a group for official communications among us and the Air Force, an aircrew scheduling group for daily schedules, an aircrew informal group, and a transportation group to let pilots and sensors know when cars or vans were going to and from the base, shopping in town, or to a restaurant.

For those with no military aviation background, even only seven days of quarantine was stressful. For me, after Survival, Evasion, Resistance and Escape (SERE) training, it was simply pampered isolation. We had WiFi available, and people would make grocery runs for us. It was just a matter of passing the time. After your seventh day of quarantine, you go to the local hospital for a COVID test. The COVID test I got in San Diego just before deploying was a throat swab. Not a big deal. The COVID test in Poland was a nasal swab. Not painful but uncomfortable. The nurse goes to the back of the sinus cavity to get the sample. It then takes a little over twenty-four hours to get the results. If you test negative, you are released from quarantine. I got my test on a Tuesday morning, got the results at noon on Wednesday, and was flying my first MQ-9 mission in Europe that afternoon. I moved out of the quarantine flat the next morning before starting my twelve-hour duty period at noon.

Our operational missions could last up to twenty-four hours and were exactly what the MQ-9 was designed to do, intelligence, surveillance, and reconnaissance (ISR) along the Western Russian border from the Baltic Sea and Kaliningrad in the north to the Black Sea and the Crimean Peninsula in the south.[14] We also supported training missions for units in the States.

During the winter months in Europe, there's often a lower level of cloud cover, but it is clear above. The fact that you couldn't see the ground didn't prevent the MQ-9 from being an effective intelligence platform. The aircraft had internal and external receivers that could monitor and relay a broad spectrum of electromatic magnetic signals to ground stations for analysis.[32] This made missions over a low-cloud deck particularly boring for the aircrew as the only control we had over the collection systems was to turn them on after takeoff and turn them off before landing. We had no ability to monitor what was being collected and, therefore, have any idea how much good we were doing.

I quickly adapted to the noon-to-midnight schedule. Fall and winter in Poland, like Germany, have lots of weather that affect and restrict flying. When we did fly, I would be done with my share of the flying on our shift by nine or ten in the evening. This meant I needed to prepare my lunch and dinner. However, if we were on weather hold or if the flight was cancelled for weather, we had the opportunity to enjoy local restaurants until Poland went into lock down for COVID about six weeks into my deployment. Then restaurants could only provide takeout dinners.

A major grocery store chain in Poland is Bedronka, which translates to "ladybug" in English. That was our go-to store for preparing our meals. The other major grocery store chain in Miroslwweic was Leviathan. Bedronka was closed on Sundays, but Leviathan was not.

Exploring the local restaurants was enjoyable and very inexpensive. Verona's and Mario's were across the parking lot from Bedronka. Mario's was a pizza place, and Verona served schnitzel and a local specialty of French fries smothered in meat and cheese, baked, and then lettuce with your choice of dressing on top. Both were ideal for a quick dine-in or takeout meal, if we were on weather hold or between shifts in the control van.

If we were on a weather hold, we had to be able to get back to the base in thirty minutes. This caused a great deal of consternation with other support personnel working for another company. They had to be at their duty station whether we were flying or not. There were other restaurants in neighboring villages that met this criterion. Three and a half miles west of Miroslaweic was the Fish House, in English rather than Polish. It had one of the most varied menus available as it was adjacent to the Park Hotel and catered to tourists. It was the unofficial after-hours hangout as several of our staff, the active-duty Air Force, and others stay at the Park Hotel rather than in the flats. Six miles further west was the Kingston restaurant in Kalisz Pomorski and still within thirty minutes of the base. This was the preferred Italian restaurant with pizza, lasagna, and a particularly good spaghetti carbonara. The Steak House Grill, nineteen miles north of Kalisz Pomorski in Drawsko Pomorskie, served steaks and ribs. This was beyond the thirty-minute radius and required a weather cancellation for us to be able to go there.

The Castle is fourteen miles south of Miroslaweic in Tuczno. It's within the thirty-minute ring. It's a nice sit-down restaurant best visited after a weather cancellation. They serve a good pork chop, duck, salmon, and have a great goulash entrée.

The city of Walcz, eighteen miles to the east of Miroslaweic, was within the thirty-minute ring and had several restaurants we enjoyed. Devran served shish kabab for either dine in or takeout. Bamboo served chicken like KFC but better as well as pizza and pasta. The Warka bar served pizza and chicken. Next door, a coffee shop served desserts and ice cream as well as coffee, a great place to end an evening.

Finally, Pila, the big city in the region, is seventeen miles east of Walcz and an hour's drive from Miroslaweic. A weather cancellation was required to get there. Pila has two major indoor shopping malls like anything in the States and the Polish equivalent of Walmart called Kaufland. Ed Jack's Truck serves very good hamburgers, and there is a sushi restaurant. The nicest restaurant, with an elegant atmosphere, is Molino's, also with a varied menu. Pila is big enough to have American spillovers like KFC and McDonalds. We avoided both.

I found it odd that even though the only reason for an American presence on the base was the MQ-9 operation, General Atomics was not the prime contractor. Huntington Ingles Industries (HII), was the prime contractor, and we were a subcontractor to them. At first, I thought this was a needless, extra layer of management but soon realized the practicality of the arrangement. Perhaps the biggest support function HII provides is housing for all contractor personnel as there is no US military billeting office. HII also handled transportation and rented all the vehicles needed to support the operation. Additionally, we needed twenty-four-hour on-site weather support. The Air Force provided one forecaster for twelve hours a day, while HII provided a forecaster for the other twelve hours. Operationally, HII coordinated all our airspace requirements and filed our international flight plans to support the tasking from the Air Force Air Operations Center (AOC). These are areas that General Atomics does not handle, nor do they want to, as their service contract is to provide aircraft, pilots, and maintenance personnel to meet the operational tasking from the Air Force. This arrangement did lead to some tensions between the HII mission planners and the flight crews. The HII personnel had to be at their workplace for their entire shift and could not get off base for a meal, even if we were on a weather hold or had cancelled flying for weather like the aircrews could. The HII personnel at times did not fully understand our operational limitations for weather. They also did not seem to appreciate we were as frustrated as they were with weather delays and mission cancellations because of the typical winter weather in Poland and our operating areas.

While I was in Poland, Tegal Airport, to the northwest of Berlin, closed, so my departure was out of Berlin Brandenburg, to the southeast of Berlin. Including layovers between flights, it took twenty-nine hours to fly from Berlin to Frankfurt, to San Francisco, to San Diego, but it all occurred on December 23 because of time zone changes going west. We took off from Frankfurt at two fifteen in the afternoon and landed in San Francisco at four fifteen that same afternoon after a ten-hour flight. Interestingly, after we took off, it got dark as we went north of the Artic Circle on our polar route and then got to be daylight again as we came south through Canada.

Routing to Poland
(Photo courtesy of ForeFlight, A Boeing Company)

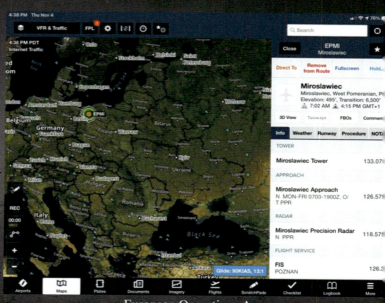

European Operations Area
(Photo courtesy of ForeFlight, A Boeing Company)

Housing Area

Housing Area First Snow

My Apartment Building

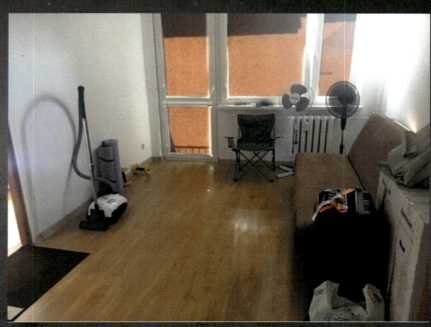

Livingroom

69

Kitchen

Bedroom

Polish Safeway

Polish 7-11

Shopping Mall

Hamburger Stand at Mall

Marijuana Vending Machine at Mall

The Castle Restaurant and Hotel

YUMA

The trip to Yuma was certainly the easiest travel-to-site I've had. I picked up a rental car in San Diego the morning of my deployment, went back to my condo, had lunch, put my bags in the car, and headed east on I-8 for the two-hour drive from San Diego to Yuma. On top of that, the living arrangement was the best yet. They call it the Towneplace Suites. The "suite" was a single room with a bed in one corner, a bathroom in one corner, a workstation in another corner, and a full kitchen in the last corner, but it was all mine—no roommate like Iraq and Poland and no tentmates like Africa. In addition to the kitchen, there was a community gas grill on the patio next to the swimming pool—a very enjoyable accommodation.

COVID was still an issue during this deployment, so new arrivals had to go into a seven-day quarantine before starting work. We felt the effects of the efforts to get people vaccinated while I was on this deployment. First, the Marines cancelled the requirement to wear face masks on base, and then people who were fully vaccinated did not have to spend seven days in quarantine before going to work. Prior to COVID, our normal deployments were ninety days long. Because of the quarantine requirements, our deployments were lengthened to 105 days to allow the replacement time to quarantine before going to work and relieving the person he or she was replacing. During this deployment, our company schedulers reflowed future deployments back to ninety days because the quarantine requirement was being eliminated. What this meant for me, for example, is that my next deployment originally scheduled for the day before Christmas to the middle of April moved to be starting in the middle of November and ending the last day of February, requiring me to again be deployed and away from family on Thanksgiving *and* Christmas.

Our customer for this site was the United States Marine Corps Unmanned Aerial Vehicle Squadron 1 (VMU-1) located on Marine Corps Air Station (MCAS) Yuma, Arizona. There are four UAV squadrons in the Marine Corps, and VMU-1 was the only one flying the MQ-9 Reaper at the time. [17, 18, 19, and 20]

The operation was a contractor-owned, contractor-operated situation with the assets leased by the Marine Corps. During my deployment, Marine and contractor pilots and sensor operators flew the MQ-9 from a control van on MCAS Yuma.[33] The Marines are very guarded about their operations, and the best open-source information from them is an article published in the Defense Visual Information Distribution Service. The aircraft are located at and launched from an "undisclosed" forward operating base (FOB) in the US Navy's 5th Fleet area of responsibility (AOR) of US Central Command (CENTCOM),[15] even though we file an unclassified international flight plan for each daily flight. The flight plan names the base where the flights originate and terminate. According to the CENTCOM webpage, the 5th Fleet AOR includes the Arabian Gulf, also called the Persian Gulf; the Gulf of Oman; the Red Sea; and parts of the Indian Ocean.[16, 21] Crews at the FOB launched and, once airborne, handed the Reaper off to the mission crews in Yuma. Once the mission is over, the mission crews return to the FOB and transfer control of the aircraft back to the landing crew for the recovery.

Except for our instrument procedure departure from and our instrument procedure arrival to, the forward operating base, all our flights were conducted in international airspace over the high seas in visual meteorological conditions (VMC) using visual flight rules (VFR) under the provisions of "due regard." The Chicago Convention of 1944 is an international agreement that established the International Civil Aviation Authority (ICAO) that publishes regulations for flight operations in international airspace as agreed to by the 193 member states. A provision in Article 3 states that "there must be 'due regard for the safety of navigation of civil aircraft' when flight is not being conducted under ICAO flight procedures." The Federal Aviation Administration defines due regard as "a phase of flight wherein an aircraft commander of State-operated aircraft assumes responsibility to separate his/her aircraft from all other aircraft."[22] A state-operated aircraft is a military or government aircraft, not a civil aircraft, such as an airliner. To operate under due regard, the FAA order and a Department of Defense instruction require the flight to be conducted in VMC and in communication with a surface radar facility that can provide flight following to ensure safe separation from other aircraft.[23] We usually had flight following from two radar facilities, one a US military site and the other the civilian air traffic control (ATC) facility for the areas in which we operated. The military facility communicated with us through a secure channel, and the civilian agency talked to us over the radio. It was amazing to me to be sitting in a control van in Arizona and talking on the radio to air traffic controllers in the Middle East.

In addition, we monitored all internationally agreed emergency frequencies in compliance with international airspace policy. If an aircraft has an emergency and doesn't know a frequency to use to contact a controlling agency, the pilot can go to one of the two emergency frequencies and call for help. Conversely, if a radar facility sees a problem or conflict between aircraft that are not on the controller's discrete frequency, he or she can make a call to advise aircraft in the area of an urgent situation. Further, if an aircraft in international airspace gets near a country's sovereign airspace without a clearance, radar facilities in that country can call on the emergency frequency to warn the aircraft and ask the pilot to identify themselves. This is called hailing the aircraft. All radio communications were in English as that is the agreed international language of aviation as established by the Chicago Convention and ICAO.

Unlike other countries, where the powers that be altered the schedule for the twenty-hour flights almost daily to try to outguess the weather, the Marines understood the value of consistency for the aircrews and maintenance. The schedule here was like an airline. We tried, usually successfully, to start the sixteen-hour mission at the same time each day, seven days a week. The night crews would fly the first eight hours of the flight, and the day crews would fly the last half of the flight. Our normal complement for an operation like this would be two day-crews, pilots and sensors, and two night-crews, with each crew splitting flying time on their shift. We maintained this manning, even though Marine pilots and sensors were flying with us.

The mission profile was equally well organized, with a standard set of coastal facilities and maritime activities to monitor on each flight. As always, we coordinated our airborne activities with a CENTCOM 5th Fleet integrated targeting center (ITC) representative.

Because of COVID, the Marines asked us to schedule only one contractor crew at a time on a shift to minimize exposure for the Marines and the General Atomics crews. To accommodate this, the GA crews on each shift alternated flying days. One day/night crew would work two days with the other crew on standby off base. Then we would switch, and the first crew would be on standby for the next two days, while the other crew flew with the Marines. Most days we had Marine pilots and sensors to share the flying time with, but on some days, no Marines were scheduled, so the GA crew flew for the entire eight hours of their shift. I was on the day shift and packed lunch each day. I used that to mark the halfway point of my shift. I started off using the traditional brown paper bag but broke down and bought a nice insulated Igloo soft lunch bag.

A major difference between this site doing remote split operations and sites where the mission crews were colocated with the launch-and-recovery crews was coordination with the customer. At sites like Iraq, Niger, and Poland, where the crews were colocated, the launch-and-recovery crews did the majority of coordination with the customer in deciding whether to fly or abort the mission because of weather or maintenance issues. The issue was usually weather as the reliability of the aircraft is amazing. Understandably, for a twenty-hour mission, conditions could change, and an early decision to cancel could miss a useful window later in the planned mission time, so crews would be on standby for extended periods, waiting for the weather to improve or for maintenance to fix the problem with the aircraft, control van, or satellite relay. Conversely, the weather could be good at the start of the mission window time, but approaching weather could make launching a risky situation for recovery options. As a mission pilot at those other locations, the go/no-go decision had already been made, and once I started flying, all I had to do was follow the taskings we were assigned, monitor the weather in the working area and the weather between the working area and the operating base. Decisions to terminate a mission early for weather or mechanical issues were very straightforward. At Yuma, the mission crews dealt directly with the Marine operations center at Yuma for all decisions, from prelaunch to in-flight. Being the only company pilot on a shift made that pilot the decision-maker in coordination with the Marines.

The Marines were a joy to work with, quintessentially professional and importantly attentive and responsive to our inputs regarding operational decisions while being mission-oriented. There was an atmosphere of mutual trust, which made for a great work environment. When I was a contractor working as the chief test pilot in the F-15 flight simulator program for Hughes, Raytheon, Link and L3, our Air Force taskmasters frequently did not trust us, thinking we were trying to get away with something or not do something they thought we should do that was not in the contract. The tension could be palpable. The frustrating thing was that most of us were former military and wanted the best for the program and the F-15 pilots who used the simulator as much as the government representatives.

Another significant difference of having the launch crew in one location and the mission crew in a different location was the fact that the mission crews in Yuma were responsible for taking control of the aircraft in the handoff from the launch crew to the control by the mission crew. This was also true for the handoff by the mission crew to the recovery crew.

The process to transfer from one control station in the Middle East to another control station in Arizona is in some ways very straightforward, but it does require considerable attention to detail and a strict protocol for the transfer. The process is somewhat intimidating when you are first exposed to it because the consequences of a misstep are attention-getting, even though there are safety features built into the system in case the station gaining control has any problems.

The day schedule in Yuma, which I was on, was the night schedule in the Middle East, and the last half of the daily mission. This meant I was always responsible for the recovery and transferring control of the aircraft from the mission control station to the recovery control station. The experienced pilots in Yuma made sure I was thoroughly checked out and comfortable with the process before turning me loose on my own for the recoveries. Additionally, there was a possibility, and it did happen, where the launch for the mission, normally handled by the other shift, could be delayed for more than eight hours, meaning our shift would also have to gain control of the aircraft from the launch crew to fly the shortened mission and then recover the aircraft as well. Because this possibility existed, I also needed to be checked out on the procedure to receive control of the aircraft from the launch crew. This necessitated my coming in on the night shift and practicing the procedure to gain control of the aircraft. As soon as I had gained control of the aircraft, I got out of the seat to let the regular night shift mission pilot fly the first half of the mission before the other day shift pilot came in to complete the mission. I did that on three different nights before I was cleared to do the procedure on my own, if needed.

In addition to the gaining and losing control procedures, I needed to be checked out on procedures for flying in our area of responsibility (AOR). This included interacting with civilian air traffic controllers as well as tactical military control and tasking. Both environments were straightforward and easy to pick up.

The communications capabilities of the MQ-9 continually amaze me. They allow me to talk to air traffic controllers in the area where the aircraft is flying. For the controller, I am virtually in the aircraft in his or her airspace in the Middle East. Once again, unlike the United States, the civilian air traffic controllers in our operating area were perfectly comfortable having us in the same airspace with commercial airliners. They used well-defined vertical and lateral separation criteria that kept all the operations safe. More than once, I heard the air traffic controller point out our location to a civilian airliner as we roamed the airspace at our assigned altitude. The controllers also advised us of civilian traffic in our area.

Military tactical control and tasking was handled through a secure channel. As always, a controller in the integrated targeting center (ITC) told us where to go and what to look at. As the pilot, I was responsible for getting the aircraft into a position where the sensor could monitor the target with either the day-TV electro-optical camera or the infrared camera used exclusively at night. I coordinated the necessary airspace with the civilian air traffic controller. All the civilian air traffic controllers were very accommodating in letting us go where we wanted in their airspace.

On days when I was on stand by and didn't fly, I made use of the kitchen in my room and prepared my meals. On days when I flew, I packed a lunch and then treated myself to dinner at a restaurant. All the standard chain restaurants were available, and I tried to avoid them, looking instead for family-owned, local establishments. There were a multitude of Mexican restaurants, and in fact, one of the best Mexican seafood restaurants I know of is in Yuma, Mariscos Mar Azul (Blue Ocean Seafood is my best translation). This may seem out of place until you look at a map and see how close Yuma is to the Gulf of California. In the 1800s, the Colorado River was navigable by river steamboats from the gulf to Yuma. Puerto Penasco, Mexico, on the north end of the gulf, is a popular spring-break location for university students in Southern California and Arizona.

A major historical site is the Yuma Territorial Prison Park and Museum. The prison was active from 1876 to 1909 and over its thirty-three-year history, before Arizona became a state, housed over three thousand inmates. Labor to build the prison was provided in part by convicts who would serve their sentences there.

Yuma Proving Grounds, just north of the city, is where the Army tests many systems in a desert environment. It's also where the Golden Knights parachute team does their winter training before starting the air show circuit each year.

The Imperial Sand Dunes are located just west of Yuma on the California side of the Colorado River. This is the largest area of sand dunes in California, about forty miles long and five miles wide, and they attract many off-highway vehicle (OHV) enthusiasts year-round but predominately in the winter months. The population of Yuma doubles with "snowbirds" during the winter months. People can camp anywhere on Bureau of Land Management lands. RV trailers and dune buggies in the middle of nowhere are prolific, with people "dry" camping, no hook ups orormal trailer parks.

Just west of the sand dunes is the town of El Centro and Naval Air Station (NAS) El Centro. The Blue Angels do their winter workups at NAS El Centro before starting their show season.

The first air show each spring for the Golden Knights away from their winter training base is usually the MCAS Yuma air show in late January or early February. NAS El Centro hosts an open house airshow in late January or early February as well, and it is the first public airshow of the year for the Blue Angels.

MCAS Yuma

Fifth Fleet Area of Operations
(Photo courtesy of ForeFlight, A Boeing Company)

CHAPTER 7

Fall/Winter 2021

FOREIGN MILITARY SALES

Companies that produce a product or provide a service want to have as many customers as possible. Defense contractors are no exception, and the ability to get Defense and State Department approval to sell products or services to other countries expands the market dramatically.

As of this writing, according to Wikipedia, General Atomics provides MQ-9s and related services to thirteen countries: Australia, Belgium, Dominican Republic, France, Germany, India, Italy, Netherlands, Spain, United Kingdom, United Arab Emirates, Taiwan, and Japan.

I got an early start on all the predeparture administrative details for my scheduled November deployment to India to fly the Sea Guardian version of the MQ-9 for the Indian Navy at Indian Naval Station Ratali, near the east coast of Southern India, near Arkonnam, a little inland from Chennai.[24]

On previous deployments, these tasks seemed to get done at the last minute. This time I had my pre-deployment physical exam, pre-deployment dental exam, pre-deployment eye exam, and new FAA second-class medical certificate completed two months before my departure date. The only things left to accomplish were a trip to GA-ASI's flight operations facility to update my currency flying the MQ-9 and the required COVID test no earlier than ninety-six hours before my flight to India via London and Doha, Qatar.

Then a month before my scheduled departure, I got the call from my boss telling me that General Atomics no longer needed my services, along with several other pilots and sensors. Seems the military has solved some of their personnel management issues in the drone force and the need for contract pilots and sensors has been dramatically reduced. I was looking forward to going to India, but the good news was I'd now be home for Thanksgiving and Christmas. I was planning to leave General Atomics after this deployment, so another benefit was that I qualified for unemployment insurance. I am now fully retired until something else fun and interesting presents itself.

EPILOGUE

I need to explain the title of this book as it causes some heartache in the drone community. It was chosen as an attention-getter. The idea obviously came from the play on words for the TV series, also because we called the conflict in Vietnam the Southeast Asia War Games since, like the conflict in the Middle East, Congress never declared either activity a "war." However, the title does cause consternation in the drone community because many people not involved in flying RPAs equate flying them to playing a video game. Nothing could be further from the truth. It is a deadly serious business, and the crews flying drones are trained professionals like any manned aircraft aircrew members. *On Killing Remotely*, a book by retired Lt. Col. Wayne Phelps, United States Marine Corps, provides an in-depth and scholarly look at the training required and the psychological impact to pilots and sensor operators flying RPAs.

This book is not intended to be scholarly. It is simply an account of my personal experience and impressions.

My three and a half years with General Atomics were rewarding and satisfying. I appreciated the opportunity afforded me. Some might look at it as a way through midlife crisis, but I got to get back into the action and help with our national defense efforts. In addition to some interesting deployments, I was able to greatly increase my retirement accounts, purchase a new car, and get a type rating in an L-39 jet trainer. I also got to travel to some interesting places I would never have paid my money to visit.

I had two objectives when I applied for this job: The first was to gain insight into drone operations, and the second was to get a better understanding of our military activities overseas.

What I learned about flying drones was enlightening and fun. I have commented several times on the adaptability and ability of other countries to integrate unmanned aircraft into their national airspace with manned, commercial activities. Here in the United States, the Federal Aviation Administration (FAA) is far behind their international counterparts. Granted, the need, and hence the urgency, is not as great, but the FAA has had the opportunity to see and appreciate the efforts of others. Yes, in Iraq and Syria, the military pretty much ran the airspace, but they still had to coordinate with civilian air traffic control. In Niger and Mali, all military operations were coordinated with civilian activity, and we operated from a joint-use airport that was the main international airport for civilian airliners going to and from Niamey, the capitol of Niger. In Poland, we operated from a military air base but dealt directly with civilian air traffic controllers in all the countries we flew in using a civilian international flight plan. Likewise, when deployed to Yuma, although all our flights in the Middle East were in international airspace, it was in radar-controlled airspace with civilian controllers from the various countries near which we operated, with the exception of Iran.

Cockpit procedures and flight operations are as complicated as a commercial jet, if not more so. Not only do you have the standard checklists for preflight, start, taxi, takeoff, climb, cruise, descent, before landing and shutdown for the MQ-9, but also, before you ever start the aircraft, you must first preflight and configure the ground control station with equally intricate checklists. The configuration checklists require extreme attention to detail because, like all computers, if you mistype anything in the required information field or enter it in the wrong sequence, nothing will work, drawing immediate attention and criticism from supervisors and customers. Once airborne, you are expected to proficiently fly using the same rules and procedures for commercial manned aircraft.

It will be interesting to see how unmanned aircraft develop as artificial intelligence is integrated into them. I don't know that any die-hard fighter pilot can foresee algorithms that will replace the man in the cockpit. Maybe there have been improvements since Bobby Fisher beat IBM's Big Blue, but only a human can think outside the box.

What I learned about our military operations with drones confirmed that no matter how well intended, reporters don't get it right either because of political bias or just plain ignorance.

I sometimes had trouble understanding what I was trying to accomplish because of security classification levels. This meant that on many occasions, they would task us to look at a building or other target by giving us coordinates and a description of the target, but they couldn't tell us why we were monitoring the target or what they were looking for. Often they had a better view of "the big picture" and would try to drive our aircraft for us rather than telling us the objectives and letting us figure out the best profile to fly.

The MQ-9 is a medium altitude surveillance platform. One time, when I was hours from home, they wanted me to drop down to a very low level to get a better view and resolution on the target, the problem being it would greatly increase my vulnerability and my fuel consumption, which would drastically reduce the time I could stay on station and monitor the target. Our taskmasters did not realize the consequences of their request.

Our taskmasters had little or no sense of flight-planning. We would be given a list of targets to monitor on our flight with no regard to a logical sequence for an efficient flight path. At one location, we had a standard landing time that was published in the daily tasking order, and yet we were constantly asked during the flight how much more time we had before we had to return to base, even though our flight path was completely predictable.

For contract pilots and sensors, our twelve-hours-on, twelve-hours-off schedule, seven days a week, was demanding while we were deployed, but it only lasted for three or four months, and we were on the same shift for the entire deployment. Then we were off for three of four months, giving us time to decompress and relax. Military crews, on the other hand, must maintain a 24/7 schedule, 365 days a year, here in the States or at their deployed location. They only worked eight-hour shifts, but they rotated shifts periodically to make sure everyone got an equally bad deal having to work all three shifts, usually 0800–1600, 1600–2400, and 0000–0800 (day, swing, and graveyard). Rotating shift work for three years is physically and mentally demanding. A military scheduler's life is a constant effort to make sure everyone gets their fair share of good deals as well as bad deals.

My thanks to the people who encouraged me to write this book and share my experiences. My hope is you found it worth your time to gain some insight into the world of military drone operations.

Appendix 1

REFERENCES

1. https://www.inherentresolve.mil/
2. https://en.wikipedia.org/wiki/Operation_Inherent_Resolve
3. https://www.eur.army.mil/Imagery/igphoto/2002230729/
4. https://safety.army.mil/ON-DUTY/Workplace/Personal-Protective-Equipment
5. https://www.airforcemag.com/usaf-colonel-on-night-of-al-asad-attack-i-didnt-believe-anyone-would-survive/
6. https://www.military.com/daily-news/2020/04/22/emotions-and-chaos-air-force-releases-eyewitness-accounts-al-asad-missile-attack.html
7. https://en.wikipedia.org/wiki/General_Atomics_MQ-1_Predator
8. https://en.wikipedia.org/wiki/Diori_Hamani_International_Airport
9. https://www.nato.int/cps/en/natohq/topics
10. https://www.airforcetimes.com/news/your-air-force/2019/03/05/air-force-mq-9-reaper-drones-based-in-poland-are-now-fully-operational/
11. https://en.wikipedia.org/wiki/Miros%C5%82awiec
12. https://www.voanews.com/africa/official-niger-facing-existential-threat
13. https://www.voanews.com/africa/us-confirms-deployment-armed-drones-niger
14. https://theaviationist.com/2020/11/12/u-s-mq-9-reaper-drones-stationed-in-poland-spotted-with-new-sigint-wing-mounted-pod/
15. https://www.dvidshub.net/news/393848/marine-corps-mq-9-reaches-10-thousand-flight-hours-central-command
16. https://www.centcom.mil/MEDIA/NEWS-ARTICLES/News-Article-View/Article/2317818/navcent-fifth-fleet-cmf-welcome-new-commander/#:~:text=The%20U.S.%205th%20Fleet%20area%20of%20operations%20encompasses%20about%202.5,parts%20of%20the%20Indian%20Ocean.
17. https://www.3rdmaw.marines.mil/Units/MAG-13/VMU-1/
18. https://www.mag14.marines.mil/Units/VMU-2/
19. https://www.1stmaw.marines.mil/Subordinate-Units/Marine-Aircraft-Group-24/VMU-3/
20. https://www.marforres.marines.mil/Major-Subordinate-Commands/4th-Marine-Aircraft-Wing/Marine-Aircraft-Group-41/Marine-Unmanned-Aerial-Vehicle-Squadron-4/
21. https://www.centcom.mil/ABOUT-US/COMPONENT-COMMANDS/
22. FAA Order 7110.65
23. DoD INSTRUCTION NUMBER 4540.01
24. https://airpowerasia.com/2021/08/04/the-formidable-general-atomics-mq-9-reaper-for-indian-armed-forces/
25. https://www.ga-asi.com/general-atomics-aeronautical-systems-altair-passes-faa-recertification-process-for-experimental-airworthiness
26. https://www.airnav.com/airport/99CL

27. https://www.airnav.com/airport/04CA
28. https://www.ga-asi.com/ga-asi-opposes-new-chinese-agriculture-project-in-grand-forks
29. https://en.wikipedia.org/wiki/General_Atomics_MQ-1_Predator
30. https://en.wikipedia.org/wiki/General_Atomics_MQ-9_Reaper
31. https://www.af.mil/News/Article-Display/Article/1133626/11th-atks-paves-way-with-training/
32. https://www.uasvision.com/2020/11/17/mq-9s-in-poland-now-have-the-new-sigint-pod/
33. https://www.ga-asi.com/usmc-acquires-2-mq-9a-reapers

To order additional copies of this book, contact:
Xlibris
844-714-8691
www.Xlibris.com
Orders@Xlibris.com

ISBN: 978-1-6698-7668-7 (sc)
ISBN: 978-1-6698-7667-0 (e)

Print information available on the last page

Rev. date: 05/10/2023

Printed in the United States
by Baker & Taylor Publisher Services